30-SECOND
EINSTEIN

SPARTANBURG
29302
AIR MAIL
4c
UNITED STATES
UNITED STATES
THOMAS JEFFERSON
CASINO
4940
AIR

30-SECOND EINSTEIN

The 50 fundamentals of his work, life and legacy, each explained in half a minute

Editor
Brian Clegg

Contributors
Philip Ball
Brian Clegg
Leon Clifford
Rhodri Evans
Andrew May

Illustrations
Steve Rawlings

IVY PRESS

First published in the UK in 2016 by
Ivy Press
210 High Street, Lewes,
East Sussex BN7 2NS, UK
www.ivypress.co.uk

British Library Cataloguing-in-Publication Data
A CIP catalogue record for this book is available from the British Library.

ISBN: 978-1-78240-387-6

This book was conceived, designed and produced by
Ivy Press

Creative Director **Michael Whitehead**
Publisher **Susan Kelly**
Editorial Director **Tom Kitch**
Art Director **James Lawrence**
Project Editor **Jamie Pumfrey**
Editor **Charles Phillips**
Designer **Ginny Zeal**
Glossaries Text **Brian Clegg**

Typeset in Section

Printed and bound in China

10 9 8 7 6 5 4 3 2 1

CONTENTS

INTRODUCTION

Brian Clegg

It's easy to think of Albert Einstein as a lone scientific adventurer, a genius who transformed our understanding of the world. However, to quote historian of science Thony Christie, 'There are no lone geniuses; science is a collective, collaborative enterprise.' Certainly Einstein did not work in isolation, but rather built on the work of his predecessors. Yet only Newton can rival Einstein's personal contribution to physics.

Perhaps because Einstein was the first scientist to receive the level of media adulation that he did, there are frequent attempts to belittle his work. Anyone working in science communication receives a steady stream of books and articles attempting to prove Einstein wrong. And, bizarrely, when in 2013 the *Observer* newspaper published a list of the top ten physicists in history, Einstein was only fourth after Newton, Bohr and Galileo. Yet while it is true that some scientists receive media attention that is totally out of proportion to their contributions, this cannot be said of Albert Einstein.

Four Major Papers

In one year, when not even an academic, he published four papers that had a huge impact. One, which won him the Nobel Prize, established the mechanism behind the photoelectric effect. That may sound insignificant, but it fired the starting gun for quantum physics. Another established the nature of Brownian motion, in which small particles such as pollen bounce around in water – demonstrating the existence of atoms, which at the time was disputed. A third established the special theory of relativity. And the fourth built on special relativity to establish the equivalence of mass and energy, leading to the world's most famous equation: $E=mc^2$. All this occurred before Einstein went on to advance quantum physics and to explain gravity with his general theory of relativity.

P
O
S
e

Einstein was never one to go along with the crowd. He hated the regimentation of German schools, and as a teenager renounced his German citizenship. It wasn't until he was 30 that he got his first academic post. And he remained resolutely a pacifist throughout his life.

How This Book Works

Each topic is clearly and concisely explained on one page in a punchy single paragraph: the **30-Second Theory**. For an even quicker overview, there is the **3-Second Thrash** alongside – the key idea caught in a single sentence. Then the **3-Minute Thought** expands on this, addressing the consequences of a theory or drawing out a quirky, intriguing aspect of the subject. Each chapter also contains the biography of a key associate of Einstein, a fellow pioneer in the field – such as Minkowski, Bohr and Bose.

To get a picture of Einstein's work we start, in **Matter**, with his early focus on atoms and the way he used statistics to explain their behaviour. Next comes **Quantum Adventures**, in which we explore his contribution to the foundations of quantum physics before getting onto his **Special Theory of Relativity**. This account of the way the fixed speed of light changes the relationship of space and time led him to an understanding of the relationship between matter and energy that lay behind nuclear bombs and nuclear power, which we find in a chapter on the relationship between **Einstein & the World** – where you'll find a discussion of his unlikely patent for a fridge!

Next we explore in **Fighting the Quantum** how Einstein challenged his contemporaries, notably Niels Bohr, on the predictions of quantum theory, leading to Einstein unwittingly uncovering the remarkable phenomenon of quantum entanglement. This came after his masterwork, the **General Theory of Relativity**, which leads us to a transformed understanding of **Einstein's Universe**.

Aptly, Einstein's work spans a range from the very small world of atoms and quantum theory to the limits of the cosmos.

1
1
10
10
16 JEWELS

MATTER

MATTER
GLOSSARY

Avogadro's number Also known as Avogadro's constant, this specifies the number of atoms or molecules in a 'mole' of substance, based on the value for 12 grams of pure carbon. The number is approximately 6.022×10^{23}. Italian scientist Amedeo Avagadro suggested in the 19th century that the volume of a gas was proportional to the number of atoms or molecules in it; when the number was established in the 20th century it was named after him.

colloid science 'Colloid' comes from the Greek for glue, making a colloid gooey or gelatinous. Such materials are usually a suspension of insoluble particles in a different substance. Colloid science includes the movement of the suspended particles, producing Brownian motion.

convection currents When a fluid has different temperatures in different locations, the motion of the atoms or molecules in the fluid results in the faster-moving, warmer particles moving upwards and the slower, cooler particles moving downwards, producing a roughly uniform mix. The movement generated in the fluid is called a convection current and is responsible for many natural phenomena.

Dulong-Petit law In the early 19th century, French physicists Pierre Dulong and Alexis Petit discovered that the amount of heat needed to raise a mass of a solid substance by 1°C was proportional to its atomic weight – a mole of the substance required a constant amount of heat. This is the Dulong-Petit law, explained by Einstein as a result of quantized vibrations.

integer quantum spin Quantum particles have a property called 'spin' that resembles angular momentum, the 'oomph' of a spinning body, although quantum spin is not actually about a particle rotating. The size of the spin, known as the spin quantum number, is quantized: it comes in fixed units, which are defined as being 0, 1/2, 1, 3/2, etc. Fermions (particles such as electrons and quarks) have half-integer spin values like 1/2, 3/2, 5/2, etc., while bosons (force-carrying particles such as photons and gluons) have integer spins.

osmotic pressure In osmosis, two quantities of a solvent containing a dissolved substance (solute) are separated by a membrane that allows the solvent through, but not the solute. Osmosis is the process of the solvent moving from the more dilute side to the less dilute until both sides have the same dilution. This is important in biology, where solvents often cross such semi-permeable membranes. The osmotic pressure is the pressure needed to resist the movement of the solvent, reflecting the strength of the osmotic process.

plasmon A quasiparticle occurring in plasmas or metal. A plasma is typically the result of heating a gas until some of the electrons surrounding the atoms in the gas become free, resulting in a mix of electrons and positive ions. The free electrons in plasmas and metals move, conducting an electrical current. If a group of electrons are moved a small amount in one direction, then released, they will be pulled back towards their natural resting place. Like a spring, this can then oscillate, and that motion acts as if it were carried by quantum particles. Plasmons influence the material's properties – for instance, the material will be transparent to light above the frequency of vibration.

quasiparticles A number of types of vibration or excitation in solids can act as if they were quantum particles, travelling through the material. Although there is no physical particle independent of the material, these quasiparticles behave like their real equivalents. Quasiparticles include phonons (quantized, soundlike vibrations), excitons (a combination of an electron and the hole it leaves behind in a semiconductor), polaritrons (an exciton interacting with a photon), magnons (the collective action of electron spins in a crystal, responsible for permanent magnetism) and plasmons (see below left).

vitalism An early explanation of the distinction between living and non-living was that living things were animated by a 'life force'. This belief was known as vitalism, and was given as an early (incorrect) explanation of Brownian motion, where pollen grains dance around in a water suspension under a microscope.

A CONVENIENT FICTION

the 30-second theory

3-SECOND THRASH
By 1900 there was no direct evidence for atoms, and no one was sure if they were real objects or just a useful fiction.

3-MINUTE THOUGHT
In 1890 Lord Rayleigh estimated the size of atoms (strictly speaking, molecules). He spread a drop of olive oil on the surface of water, assuming that at its maximum extent the film would be one molecule thick. His estimate of 16×10^{-8} cm was close to the value Agnes Pockels obtained two years later, and also pretty close to the modern value – but still he lacked direct evidence that molecules and atoms were real at all.

The idea of atoms as the fundamental constituents of matter goes back at least as far as the Greek philosophers Leucippus and Democritus in the 5th century BCE, but there were various ways of believing it. Some, like Isaac Newton and the 18th-century Swiss scientist Daniel Bernoulli, thought of atoms as real, invisibly small particles. Others regarded them as a convenient fiction, like national boundaries: useful for thinking about natural phenomena but not a part of physical reality. By the end of the 19th century many scientists took atoms literally, but there was no direct evidence for them: they were, like dark matter today, a working hypothesis. When Ludwig Boltzmann developed his 'kinetic theory' of gases in the 1870s–90s by assuming gases are collections of frantically moving atoms, he faced opposition from sceptics of atomic theory such as Wilhelm Ostwald and Ernst Mach, who thought that energy was the fundamental stuff and that science shouldn't accept concepts that cannot be sensed directly. The criticism left Boltzmann feeling depressed and marginalized. According to Einstein's biographer Abraham Pais, 'it is hard to imagine the embattled Boltzmann evincing the serious yet playful spirit with which Einstein handled the problem of molecular reality.' Albert had the right personality to carry the idea further.

RELATED ENTRIES
See also
DETERMINING MOLECULAR DIMENSIONS
page 16

BROWNIAN MOTION EXPLAINED
page 20

PERRIN'S PARTICLES
page 24

3-SECOND BIOGRAPHIES

DEMOCRITUS
c.460–c.370 BCE
Greek philosopher, considered the 'father of atoms'

JOHN DALTON
1766–1844
English chemist who proposed modern atomic theory in 1803

ERNST MACH
1838–1916
Austrian physicist, a leading sceptic of atomic hypothesis in the early 20th century

30-SECOND TEXT
Philip Ball

John Dalton used the ancient concept of atoms to explain the behaviour of the chemical elements.

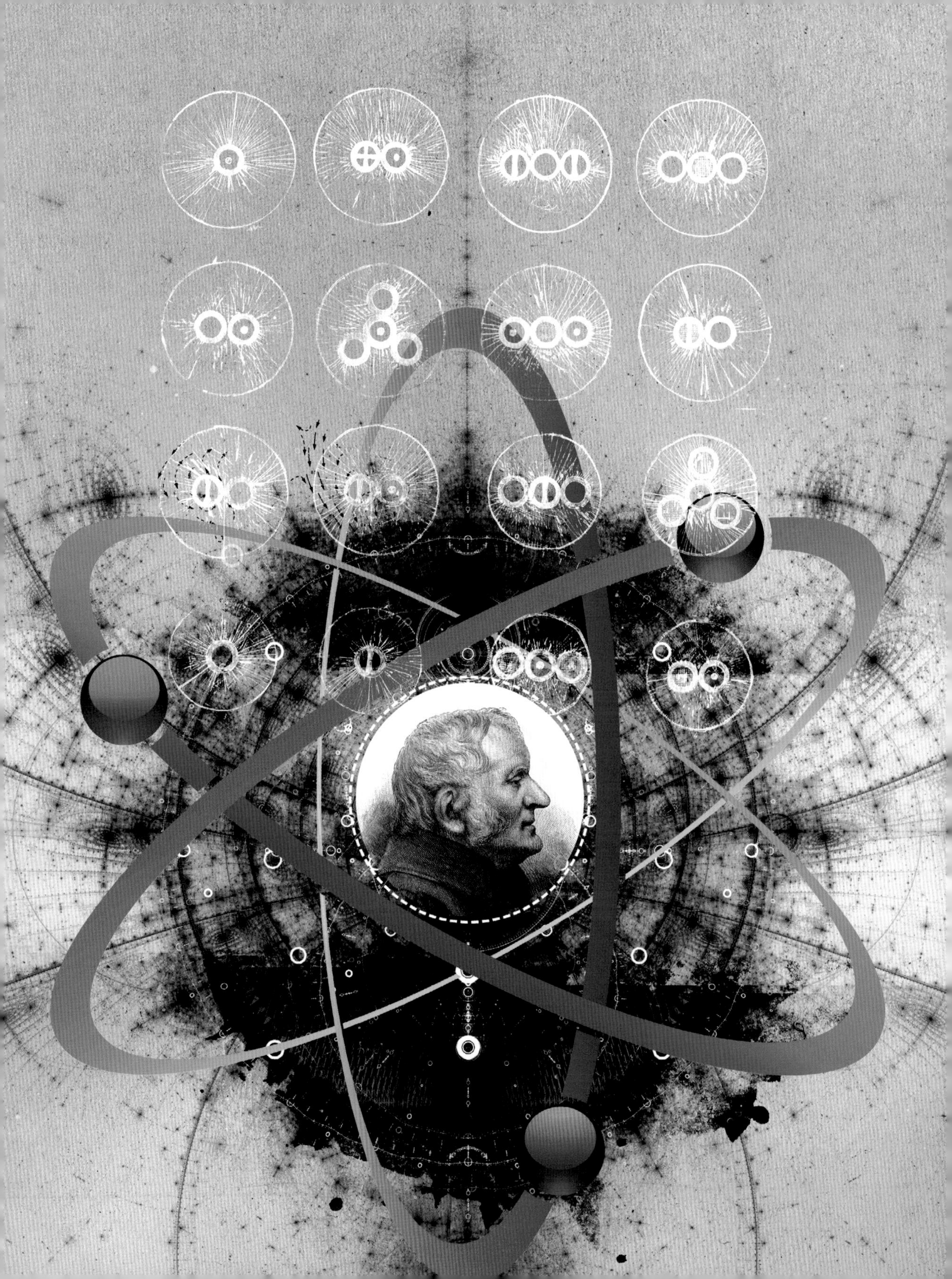

DETERMINING MOLECULAR DIMENSIONS

the 30-second theory

At the start of his career, Einstein could have been mistaken for a chemist. Much of his interest centred on atoms and molecules: how big they were, what forces acted between them, how they moved around in solids, liquids and gases. Einstein's first dissertation submitted to the University of Zurich in 1901 has been lost, and amazingly it's not known quite what was in it, although it seems to have been about molecular forces. He withdrew it in 1902, again for reasons not wholly clear, but he submitted a new one in July 1905 on a topic that he had chosen himself. Molecules again: to be precise, the thesis described a new way of estimating their size and the number of them (called Avogradro's number) contained in the chemist's universal measure of quantity of substance, the mole. His method was new and unusual, making use of the theories of fluid motion (hydrodynamics) and of solutions and osmotic pressure. It involved aspects of diffusion theory – the random, heat-driven movements of molecules and small particles – that were to resurface in his work on Brownian motion. The thesis – which Einstein also published as a paper in *Annalen der Physik* the same year – was entirely theoretical, which was risky before theoretical physics was recognized as a valid discipline. It was accepted in August.

3-SECOND THRASH
Einstein's doctoral thesis at the University of Zurich in 1905 described a new method for measuring the size of molecules – offering indirect proof that they really exist.

3-MINUTE THOUGHT
The value Einstein estimated in his thesis for the size of a sugar molecule (one nanometre, 10^{-9} m) is reasonably accurate. But his value for Avogradro's number, 2.1×10^{-23}, is three times too small. Partly that's because his calculations contained an error, which his student Ludwig Hopf pointed out in 1911. Einstein redid the calculation and got a value much closer to the one currently accepted. Even he got things wrong sometimes.

RELATED ENTRIES
See also
A CONVENIENT FICTION
page 14

ADVENTURES IN STATISTICAL MECHANICS
page 18

3-SECOND BIOGRAPHIES
ALFRED KLEINER
1849–1916
Swiss experimental physicist who acted as Einstein's doctoral adviser after he fell out with the previous one, Heinrich Weber

WILLIAM SUTHERLAND
1859–1911
Scottish-Australian physicist, said to be the greatest expert on molecular physics in his day, who in 1905 devised a method for estimating the masses of molecules that was similar to Einstein's

30-SECOND TEXT
Philip Ball

In his doctoral thesis, Einstein used the behaviour of fluids to predict the dimensions of molecules.

ADVENTURES IN STATISTICAL MECHANICS

the 30-second theory

Einstein's contributions to the understanding of the properties of matter tend to get overshadowed by his work on relativity and the fundamentals of quantum theory, but they in themselves amount to a scientific achievement of great distinction. Much of Einstein's early work in this field built on that of James Clerk Maxwell and Ludwig Boltzmann, which accounted for the bulk properties of solids, gases and liquids on the basis of the motions and forces of interaction between their atomic and molecular constituents. This was an exercise in statistics: explaining how average molecular behaviour produces tangible phenomena such as pressure and density, and the laws of thermodynamics that connect them. It showed how a mechanical worldview extended even to what then seemed to be the most fundamental description of matter. In 1902–4, Einstein published three papers that attempted to put this statistical mechanics on a firmer footing. He later merged this approach with the quantum view of atomic vibrations introduced by Max Planck to explain the 'heat capacity' of solids: how readily they absorb heat. This had long been described empirically by a relationship called the Dulong-Petit law, which Einstein's analysis of quantized vibrations in a simple model solid explained in 1907.

3-SECOND THRASH
Einstein's earliest work investigated how the observable, thermodynamic properties of matter relate to the statistics of their underlying molecular interactions and the molecular theory of heat.

3-MINUTE THOUGHT
Statistical mechanics is arguably a more fundamental part of physics than relativity or quantum theory, in that its concepts – such as the abrupt changes of state called phase transitions and the points of instability and wild fluctuation called critical points – are applied in fields ranging from nuclear physics to superconductivity, polymer physics and the motions of crowds. At root these ideas relate to how collective behaviour emerges from the interaction of many component parts.

RELATED ENTRIES
See also
DETERMINING MOLECULAR DIMENSIONS
page 16

BROWNIAN MOTION EXPLAINED
page 20

QUANTIZED VIBRATIONS
page 40

3-SECOND BIOGRAPHIES
JOSIAH WILLARD GIBBS
1839–1903
American chemical physicist whose 1902 monograph is considered the foundation of classical statistical mechanics

LUDWIG BOLTZMANN
1844–1906
Austrian physicist who pioneered the microscopic statistical theory of matter based on the atomic hypothesis

30-SECOND TEXT
Philip Ball

By using statistics, Einstein predicted the behaviour of matter as a combination of the actions of many atoms or molecules.

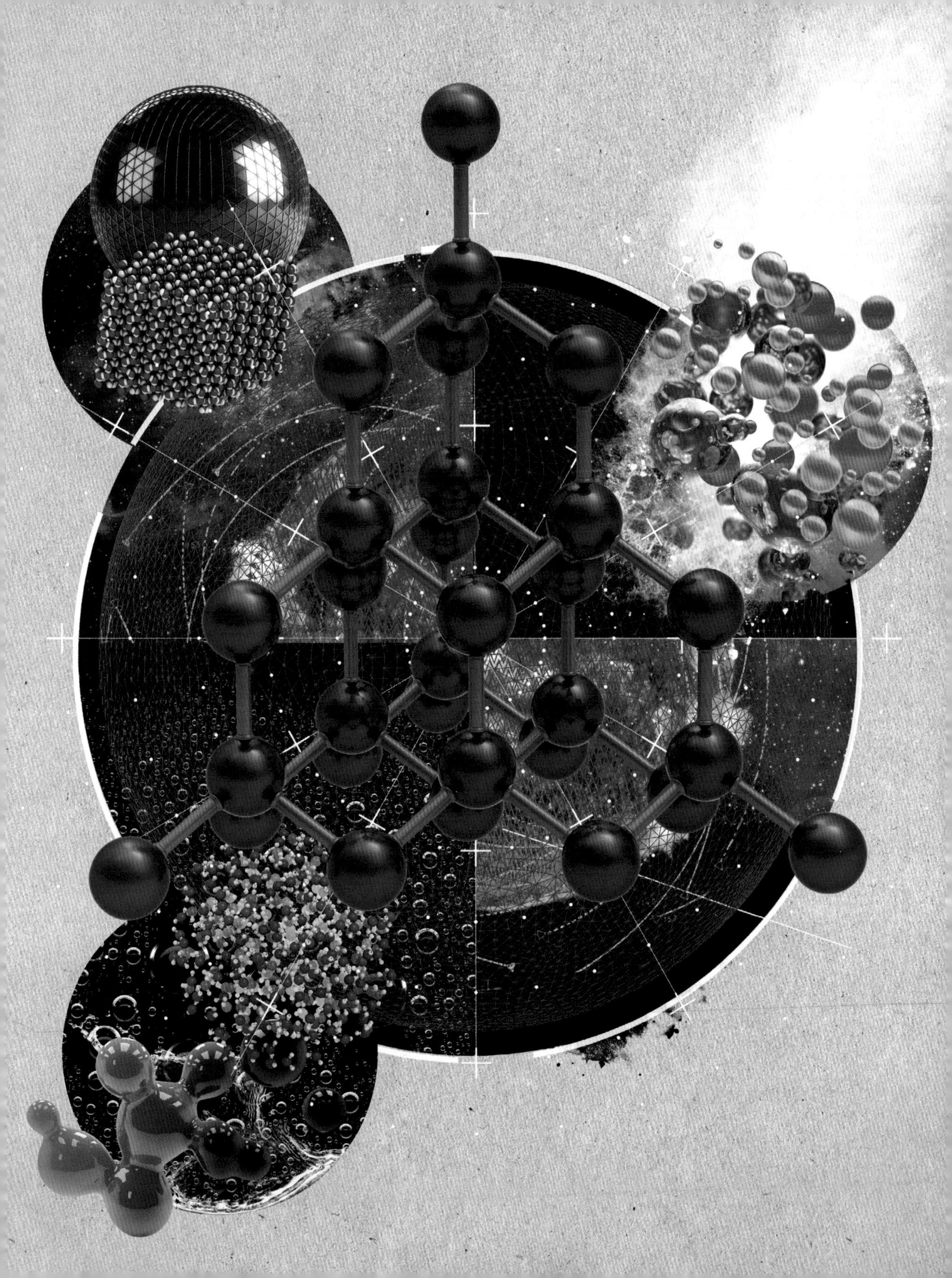

BROWNIAN MOTION EXPLAINED

the 30-second theory

When in 1828 the botanist Robert Brown saw pollen grains suspended in water dancing wildly under the microscope, he thought at first that this activity revealed the fundamental 'active force' of life embodied in the old idea of vitalism. However, he later found that inanimate grains behaved in the same way, so the jiggling could have nothing to do with life. Then what caused it? Convection currents, evaporation, electrical forces: all these and others were invoked and then dismissed as explanations over the course of the nineteenth century. In 1905 Einstein offered the first convincing explanation. For particles this small, he said, collisions with surrounding solvent molecules undergoing random thermal motion don't average out in all directions, so that the particles will be deflected this way and that. Einstein's paper, drawing on the theory that equated heat with random molecular movement, was the first thorough treatment of diffusion in a liquid. It ended by pointing out how measuring the average displacement of a grain over time could provide an estimate of the size of molecules. Conversely, he wrote, if his predictions were wrong, the whole molecular theory of heat would be called into doubt.

3-SECOND THRASH

Einstein explained the random 'Brownian' motion of small particles suspended in water in terms of their collisions with the surrounding water molecules.

3-MINUTE THOUGHT

Brownian motion is the classic example of a random walk: a path consisting of steps in a random direction. In 1900, five years before Einstein's classic paper, French physicist Louis Bachelier proposed that changes in stock and share prices correspond to what is effectively a random walk. His mathematical treatment of economic fluctuations has similarities with Einstein's work, and is often considered the founding text of 'econophysics', which uses ideas from physics to understand economics.

RELATED ENTRIES

See also
A CONVENIENT FICTION
page 14

PERRIN'S PARTICLES
page 24

3-SECOND BIOGRAPHIES

ROBERT BROWN
1773–1858
Scottish botanist whose microscopic studies of plants and cells led him to observe the erratic movements of suspended particles

LOUIS GEORGES GOUY
1854–1926
French physicist who made observations of Brownian motion that Einstein cited in 1906 as partly confirming his theory

30-SECOND TEXT
Philip Ball

The random dance of molecules in a fluid accounted for the motion of larger, visible suspended particles in the fluid .

1 January 1894
Born in Calcutta, India

1913
Obtains his BSc in applied mathematics from Presidency College, Calcutta

1915
Gains MSc in applied mathematics from Presidency College

1915
Marries Ushabati Ghosh; they had nine children, but two died in early childhood

1916
Joins the University of Calcutta as a research scholar

1919
Makes the first translation into English of Einstein's German-language papers on the special and general theories of relativity

1921
Becomes reader in the Department of Physics at the University of Dhaka

1924
Derives Planck's radiation law by treating the photons as a collection of identical particles

1924
Spends two years working in Europe in X-ray and crystallography laboratories

1926
Returns to Dhaka and is promoted to professor and made head of department

1945
Returns to Calcutta when the partition of India becomes imminent

1956
Retires and becomes emeritus professor at the University of Calcutta

1956
Becomes vice-chancellor of Viswa-Bharati University in Shanti Niketan

1958
Returns to University of Calcutta to continue with research

4 February 1974
Dies, in Calcutta, aged 80

SATYENDRA BOSE

Satyendra Nath Bose was born in Calcutta in India, the eldest and only boy of seven children. His family moved to Goabagan where he attended the New Indian School, and then the prestigious Hindu School. Bose came fifth in the entrance exams to Presidency College (Calcutta), and decided to study intermediate science, specializing in applied mathematics. He obtained his BSc in 1913 and his MSc (also in applied mathematics) in 1915, graduating top of his class on both occasions. Due to these exceptional achievements, in 1916 he was appointed a research scholar at the University of Calcutta.

He became interested in the two emerging fields of quantum mechanics and relativity, and in 1919 he made the first English translation of some of Einstein's papers, which had originally been published in German. In 1921 he moved to become reader in the department of physics in Dhaka (now in Bangladesh); in 1924 he derived Planck's radiation law using an entirely new method of assuming photons are indistinguishable particles, developing a new statistics to describe such particles. His paper was not accepted by any journal, so he sent his work to Einstein who immediately recognized its importance and translated it into German to be published in *Zeitschrift für Physik*. With Einstein's support, Bose moved to Europe for two years and worked with many of the great physicists of the day, such as Marie Curie and Louis de Broglie.

In 1926 he returned to Dhaka, and with Einstein's backing and recommendation was promoted to professor, despite his not having a PhD. He soon became head of department, and remained in Dhaka until the partition of India became imminent, when he decided to leave what would become Bangladesh to return to Calcutta. He remained at the University of Calcutta until his retirement in 1956, but was soon persuaded out of retirement to become vice-chancellor of Visva-Bharati University in Shanti Niketan, West Bengal. Two years later he returned to work on his research at Calcutta until his death in 1974 at the age of 80.

Rhodri Evans

PERRIN'S PARTICLES

the 30-second theory

Einstein's 1905 paper on the random 'Brownian' motion of small particles suspended in water ended with a prediction of how far, on average, they would travel in a given time. For a grain 1 micrometre (1/1000th of a millimetre) across, this distance would be about 6 micrometres in a minute at around room temperature. 'Let us hope,' Einstein said, 'that a researcher will soon succeed in solving the problem.' But it was a tough challenge, demanding very careful observations using a microscope. Fortunately, the means had just been invented. In 1902 Richard Zsigmondy, working for the Schott Glass company in Jena, described a new device called an ultramicroscope that, by directing strong light beams onto a sample, could reveal Brownian motion with great clarity. By 1906 others were trying to use it to test Einstein's theory. None was as adept as the Frenchman Jean Perrin, working at the Sorbonne in Paris, whose measurements of the motions of grains of the pigment gamboge, prepared with precise particle sizes, in 1908 bore out Einstein's predictions. Einstein was delighted – he had not expected experiments to have the required precision so soon. Perrin was awarded the 1926 Nobel Prize in physics, a year after Zsigmondy won the chemistry Nobel for his invention.

3-SECOND THRASH

In 1908 Jean Perrin used a microscope to observe and measure the Brownian motion of small particles, confirming the predictions of Einstein's theory.

3-MINUTE THOUGHT

Brownian particles belong to the field of colloid science, which is concerned with suspensions of 'medium-sized' particles – generally visible in the microscope – in some other substance, such as emulsions of oil droplets in water. Named by the Scottish chemist Thomas Graham in the early 19th century, and studied by Michael Faraday and John Tyndall, it was the first acknowledgement of a distinct 'mesoscale' world between the molecular and the macroscopic.

RELATED ENTRIES

See also
A CONVENIENT FICTION
page 14

BROWNIAN MOTION EXPLAINED
page 20

3-SECOND BIOGRAPHIES

RICHARD ZSIGMONDY
1865–1929
Austrian scientist whose ultramicroscope enabled the crucial test of Einstein's theory of Brownian motion

MARIAN SMOLUCHOWSKI
1872–1917
Polish-Austrian scientist who worked out a theory of Brownian motion independently of Einstein

30-SECOND TEXT

Philip Ball

Within three years of Einstein's predictions on Brownian motion they were confirmed by measurements made by Jean Perrin using a precision microscope.

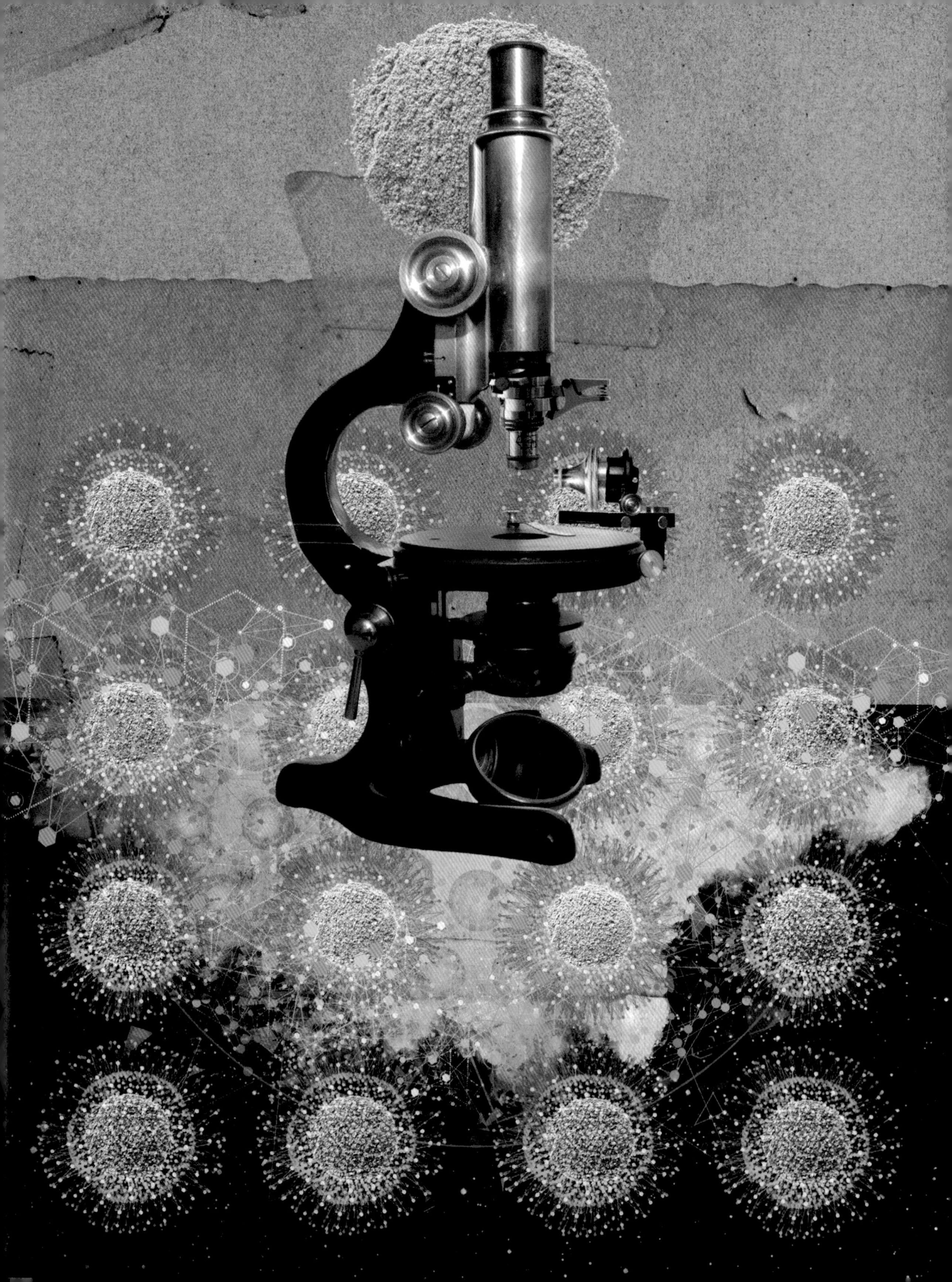

BOSE-EINSTEIN STATISTICS

the 30-second theory

3-SECOND THRASH
Indistinguishable particles, called bosons, obey different statistics to particles that we can distinguish from each other by their location and quantum state.

3-MINUTE THOUGHT
The evolution of many complex systems, including businesses, are found to follow Bose-Einstein statistics. Such statistics predict the evolution of—for example—the winner-takes-all phenomenon that is so often observed in competitive systems.

In 1924 Indian mathematician Satyendra Bose sent a paper to Einstein that had been rejected by several scientific journals. The paper dealt with a new way of counting particles that are indistinguishable from each other, such as photons. Einstein immediately recognized the paper's importance, translated it into German and got it published. We now call this way of counting indistinguishable particles Bose-Einstein statistics. Suppose we are flipping two coins, which we will initially treat as being distinguishable. The four possible outcomes are head-head (HH), head-tail (HT), tails-head (TH) and tail-tail (TT) – and so the probability of producing two heads is one in four. However, if the two coins were indistinguishable we would not be able to differentiate between the (HT) and (TH) outcomes, and so the only possible outcomes would be (HH), (TH) or (TT); the probability of producing two heads now becomes one in three. Bose showed that indistinguishable particles in physics, such as photons, obey similar statistics. We now call such indistinguishable particles 'bosons' in his honour. Particles that don't obey these statistics, including the particles that make up matter, are called fermions. Unlike bosons, fermions can't be simultaneously in the same location in the same quantum state, making them distinguishable.

RELATED ENTRIES
See also
SATYENDRA BOSE
page 22

BOSE-EINSTEIN CONDENSATES
page 28

3-SECOND BIOGRAPHIES

JAMES CLERK MAXWELL
1831–79
Scottish physicist; formulated the first statistical theory, the distributions of the speeds of particle speeds in a gas

SATYENDRA BOSE
1894–1974
Indian mathematical physicist who first derived the statistics of indistinguishable particles

ERIC CORNELL
1961–
American physicist who co-produced the first Bose-Einstein condensate

30-SECOND TEXT
Rhodri Evans

Whether or not two particles (or coins) are distinguishable determines the statistical outcome of their behaviour.

ELIZABETH II D G REG F D 2002
ELIZABETH II D G REG F D 2005
ONE PENNY
1

BOSE-EINSTEIN CONDENSATES

the 30-second theory

3-SECOND THRASH
A Bose-Einstein condensate is a state of matter in which particles coalesce, share the same single quantum state and act like one massive particle.

3-MINUTE THOUGHT
Bose-Einstein condensates can be made from disturbances or excitations in matter as well as from atoms and particles. Crucially, these excitations behave as though they are boson-like particles and are sometimes called quasiparticles. Examples include excitons in semiconductors, plasmons within plasmas and magnons in crystals. Another example is the polariton, which combines a photon of light with an exciton. In 2013, a room-temperature Bose-Einstein condensate was made from polaritons in tiny nanoscale wires.

Some scientists call Bose-Einstein condensates the fifth state of matter – joining solids, liquids, gases and plasmas. Individual atoms or separate subatomic particles condense and share a single low-energy quantum state. Bose-Einstein condensates are made from bosons, subatomic particles with integer quantum spin that obey the rules of Bose-Einstein statistics and can occupy the same quantum state. These condensates can also be made from certain atoms in which the sum of the quantum spins of their constituent particles add up to an integer, like a boson; at low temperatures or very high pressures these atoms can behave as bosons. Bose and Einstein predicted the existence of such a phenomenon in 1924. They realized that if a gas of non-interacting boson-like atoms could be cooled to a sufficiently low temperature then it would condense into a material in which all the constituent atoms shared the lowest energy quantum state. However, Bose-Einstein condensates were not made in the laboratory until 1995 by two teams of physicists who cooled atoms to near absolute zero (-273°C); one cooled rubidium atoms and the other cooled sodium atoms. In 2013, a Bose-Einstein condensate was made at room temperature within nanoscale wires.

RELATED ENTRIES
See also
SATYENDRA BOSE
page 22

BOSE-EINSTEIN STATISTICS
page 26

3-SECOND BIOGRAPHIES
WILLIAM DANIEL PHILLIPS
1948–
American Nobel Prize-winning physicist who pioneered laser cooling techniques to help make Bose-Einstein condensation a reality

ERIC CORNELL, CARL WIEMAN & WOLFGANG KETTERLE
1961–, 1951– & 1957–
Two American and one German physicists who won the 2001 Nobel Prize for making the first Bose-Einstein condensate

30-SECOND TEXT
Leon Clifford

In a B-E condensate, the fifth state of matter, particles share the lowest energy state, moving from a wide distribution of states (left) to a clear peak (middle and right).

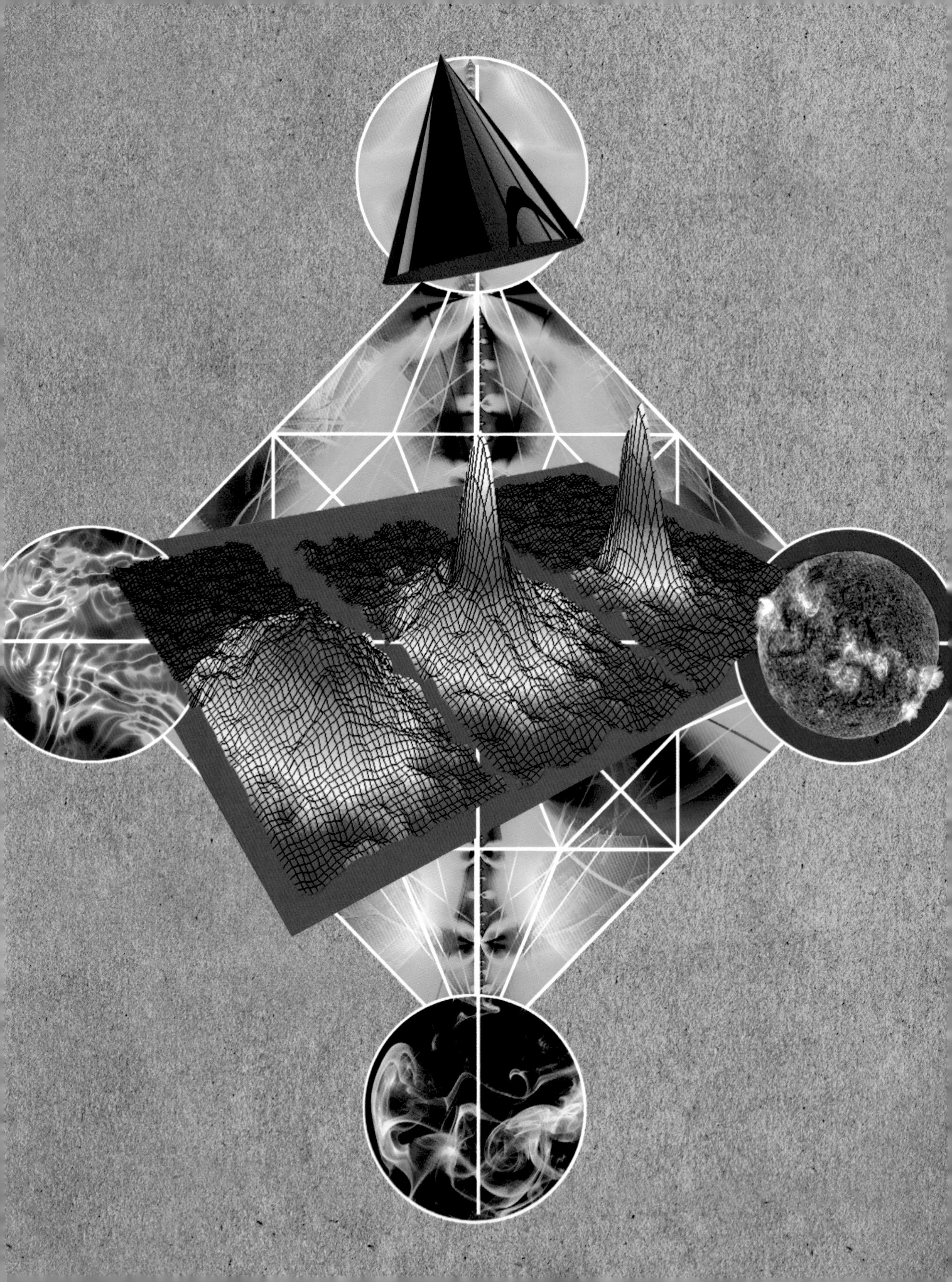

QUANTUM ADVENTURES

blackbody/blackbody radiation
A blackbody is not black, but glows with light. It is a hypothetical object that absorbs all light of any frequency that hits it, but also radiates light at all frequencies. This so-called blackbody radiation has specific characteristics: the distribution of frequencies emitted (it emits more at some frequencies than others) is always the same for a particular temperature. Many objects that glow due to being hot behave like blackbodies, but our best approximation is a cavity in a solid block with a small hole through which the radiation is emitted. It was in attempting to explain the distribution of blackbody radiation frequencies that Max Planck was forced to assume that light energy came in packets or quanta.

graininess of the quantum world
A term used to indicate the way that many physical phenomena are broken into chunks rather than being continuous. 'Graininess' is a reference to predigital photography, when the detail in a photograph depended on the size of the chemical grains in the photographic film.

photoelectric effect When light is shone on some metals or semiconductors, the light energy can be absorbed by electrons in the material. The electrons are pushed away from their atoms, making it easier for the electrons to cause an electrical current. This is the photoelectric effect. The effect requires photons of a certain energy (colour or frequency) before it will work. If the light has too low a frequency, it can't push the electrons up in energy as the energy levels are quantized: they can't take any value, but require a 'quantum leap'. Einstein's early quantum ideas explained the photoelectric effect.

Planck length The smaller the space considered, the more it is ruled by quantum effects. Make a distance small enough and quantum effects make measurement impossible. This occurs around the Planck length, which is approximately 1.616×10^{-35} metres – more than a billion billion times smaller than a proton. The value was derived as a distance unit based only on fundamental constants of nature. The Planck length is the square root of the reduced Planck constant (which relates the energy of a photon of light to the light's frequency) times the gravitational constant divided by the cube of the speed of light.

Planck's constant A fundamental constant in physics with a value of around 6.626×10^{-34} joule seconds. The Planck constant is the ratio of the energy of a photon to its frequency. Where the Planck constant is represented by *h*, there is an alternative 'reduced Planck constant' represented by an *h* with a bar across it, which is $h/2\pi$ – this is useful for applications that represent the frequency of the light in terms of a repeated rotation.

quantum world As distinct from 'classical world'. Until the 20th century, most physical phenomena were thought to be continuously variable. In this 'classical' world, for instance, we could measure a distance as small as we like, and the energy of light could have any value. However, as quantum physics developed scientists realized that much of the world is quantized – it comes in 'chunks'. For instance, we now believe that it is not possible to measure distances below the 'Planck length', and light comes in packets of energy. We inhabit a quantum world.

semiconductor A material – notably silicon and germanium – that is more conductive than an insulator like glass, and less conductive than most metals. Typically in a semiconductor, the electrons are held in a crystal lattice, but when they are excited – usually by incoming light, or an electrical current – they are pushed out of the lattice, leaving a 'hole' behind that acts like a positively charged particle. The freed electron joins the conduction layer, where it can move freely and carry a current. Semiconductors are often 'doped' – impurities are added to the lattice to increase the semiconductor's sensitivity.

EINSTEIN'S CHANGING PHYSICS

the 30-second theory

Max Planck was by nature cautious and conservative, but he transformed physics with a radical idea that won him a Nobel Prize in 1918. It concerned the question of how radiation is emitted from warm bodies: so-called 'blackbody radiation'. The wavelength of the most intense radiation gets shorter as the temperature increases: as an electric heater warms up, it first emits invisible infrared light, then red, then yellow. Previous efforts to explain the radiation in terms of atomic vibrations seemed to lead to the conclusion that the amount of energy radiated should get ever greater the shorter the wavelength, leading to an 'ultraviolet catastrophe' – where the energy became infinite. In 1900, Planck found that the equations of blackbody radiation would produce more sensible results if one assumed that the energy of the atomic vibrations was divided into packets or 'quanta' with an energy proportional to the frequency of the light. For Planck this was simply a mathematical trick – as he put it, a 'fortunate guess'. But Einstein argued that Planck's energy quanta were real – and what's more, that they applied to all energy, meaning that light itself was apportioned into discrete quanta, later called photons. At first Planck was too disturbed by this dislocation in the traditional view of light to accept the quantum hypothesis.

3-SECOND THRASH

The quantum hypothesis of Max Planck – the idea that energy comes in packets – was seized on by Einstein to fashion an entirely new kind of physics, ultimately becoming quantum

3-MINUTE THOUGHT

Planck assumed that the energy of a quantum of vibration was proportional to its frequency; he called the constant of proportionality *h*, which became known as Planck's constant. We now recognize that *h* encodes from the fundamentally grainy nature of the quantum world. The smallest meaningful measure of distance is called the Planck length, equal to 1.616×10^{-35} metres.

RELATED ENTRIES

See also
PHOTOELECTRIC QUANTA
page 36

QUANTIZED VIBRATIONS
page 40

3-SECOND BIOGRAPHIES

MAX PLANCK
1858–1947
Elder statesman of German science, who was more or less destroyed by the tribulations of the Nazi era

WILHELM WIEN
1864–1928
German experimental physicist who found mathematical relationships between a blackbody's temperature, the energy it radiates and the wavelength of its most intense radiation

30-SECOND TEXT

Philip Ball

A blackbody radiates light in a specific distribution of colours that is determined by the temperature of the body.

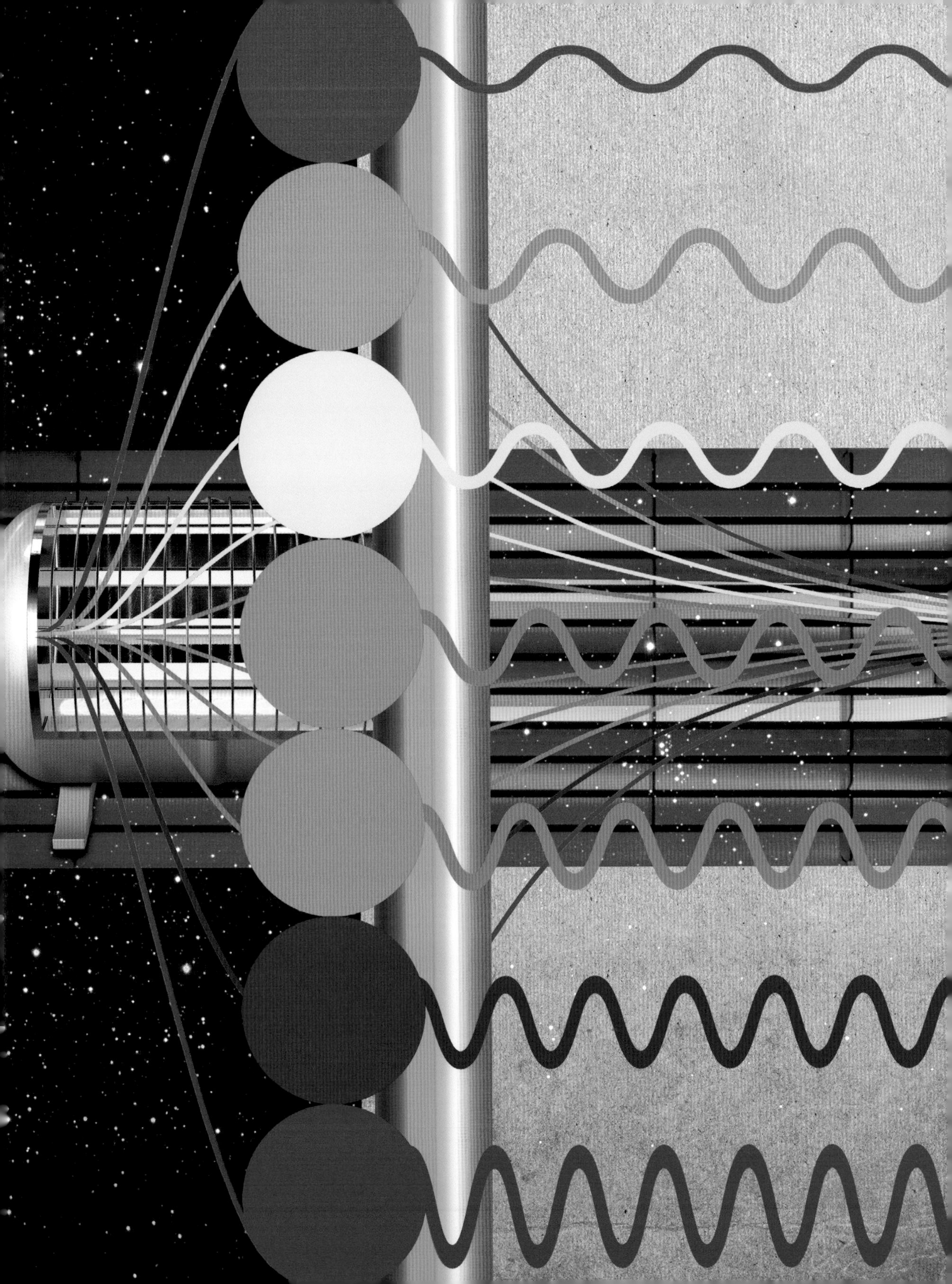

PHOTOELECTRIC QUANTA

the 30-second theory

3-SECOND THRASH
In 1905 Einstein extended the idea of light quanta proposed by Max Planck in 1900 to explain all observed properties of the photoelectric effect.

3-MINUTE THOUGHT
Photomultipliers, which were first developed in the 1930s, use the photoelectric effect to amplify faint light signals and hence enable detection of low intensity sources. They were used in early electronic image sensors in astronomy and in video cameras. Night vision devices also use the photoelectric effect: a thin film of alkali metal or a semiconductor is placed in an image intensifier tube.

In 1905, Einstein wrote a paper to explain the photoelectric effect, a phenomenon that had been puzzling physicists for several years. Experiments had shown that certain metals would emit electrons when light shone on them, but the energy of the electrons did not depend on the intensity of the light. Additionally, if the light was changed to a lower frequency, the phenomenon disappeared. All of this ran counter to the traditional wave theory of light. Building on the 1900 work of Max Planck, Einstein suggested that the light falling on the metal came in discrete chunks, 'quanta'. Planck had introduced quanta to explain emitted light from a blackbody, but Einstein generalized this and argued that the light could only interact with the electrons in discrete quanta, the energy of each quantum of light being given by Planck's equation $E=hf$, where f is the frequency of the light. This idea brilliantly explained all the observed aspects of the photoelectric effect. Einstein argued that each metal had a threshold frequency; if the frequency of the light were less than this, no photoelectric effect would be observed. In addition, the intensity of light just meant more light quanta arriving each second, which would not affect the energy of each emitted electron. This work led Einstein to be awarded his only Nobel Prize, for physics, in 1921.

RELATED ENTRIES
See also
MILLIKAN DELIVERS
page 38

TOWARDS WAVE-PARTICLE DUALITY
page 44

3-SECOND BIOGRAPHIES
ALEXSANDR STOLETOV
1839–96
Russian physicist, his analysis of the photoelectric effect derived results that Einstein's 1905 theory explained

HEINRICH HERTZ
1857–94
German physicist, the first scientist to observe the photoelectric effect in 1887

30-SECOND TEXT
Rhodri Evans

In the photoelectric effect, low energy photons have no impact, but higher energy photons displace electrons, producing an electric current.

MILLIKAN DELIVERS

the 30-second theory

3-SECOND THRASH
It took a disbeliever in Einstein's prediction that light was quantized into tiny packets to conduct the experiments that would prove the theory correct.

3-MINUTE THOUGHT
Millikan's experimental proof of Einstein's quantum theory of light neatly demonstrates the process that drives modern physics. This interaction between theorists who come up with the ideas and experimentalists who test them is vital. However, modern experimental apparatus – such as the CERN particle accelerator – is huge and expensive – and can take decades to build. As physicists delve deeper into the nature of reality, what will it take to test their theories in the future?

American physicist Robert Millikan proved Einstein's 1905 prediction that light was quantized in a series of experiments that he completed in 1916. Millikan did not accept Einstein's quantum explanation of the photoelectric effect but he saw that Einstein's photoelectric equation could be tested experimentally. Einstein's formula predicted a straight-line relationship between the frequency of the light that was used and the maximum energy of the emitted electrons. Millikan set out to test this relationship. Others had tried with inconclusive results, but Millikan was a great and skilful experimenter who went to painstaking lengths to make precise measurements. To ensure the accuracy of his experiment, Millikan required extremely clean surfaces that could only be achieved in a vacuum; he also needed to build a large and elaborate apparatus to eliminate potential experimental errors. Millikan described this complex equipment experiment as 'a machine shop in vacuo'. By carefully varying the voltages within the equipment, he was able to measure the maximum energy imparted to electrons emitted from a metal plate by light of different frequencies that was shone onto that plate and he found a straight-line relationship. Millikan won the Nobel Prize for physics in 1923 for this work and for measuring the charge on an electron.

RELATED ENTRIES
See also
PHOTOELECTRIC QUANTA
page 36

QUANTIZED VIBRATIONS
page 40

TOWARDS WAVE-PARTICLE DUALITY
page 44

3-SECOND BIOGRAPHIES
ROBERT MILLIKAN
1868–1953
American physicist who in addition to verifying Einstein's photoelectric effect won the Nobel Prize for establishing the electric charge of the electron

WILMER SOUDER
1884–1974
American physicist who was Millikan's experimental assistant in demonstrating the photoelectric effect

30-SECOND TEXT
Leon Clifford

Millikan set out to disprove that Einstein's photons existed, but instead his work confirmed the quantum prediction.

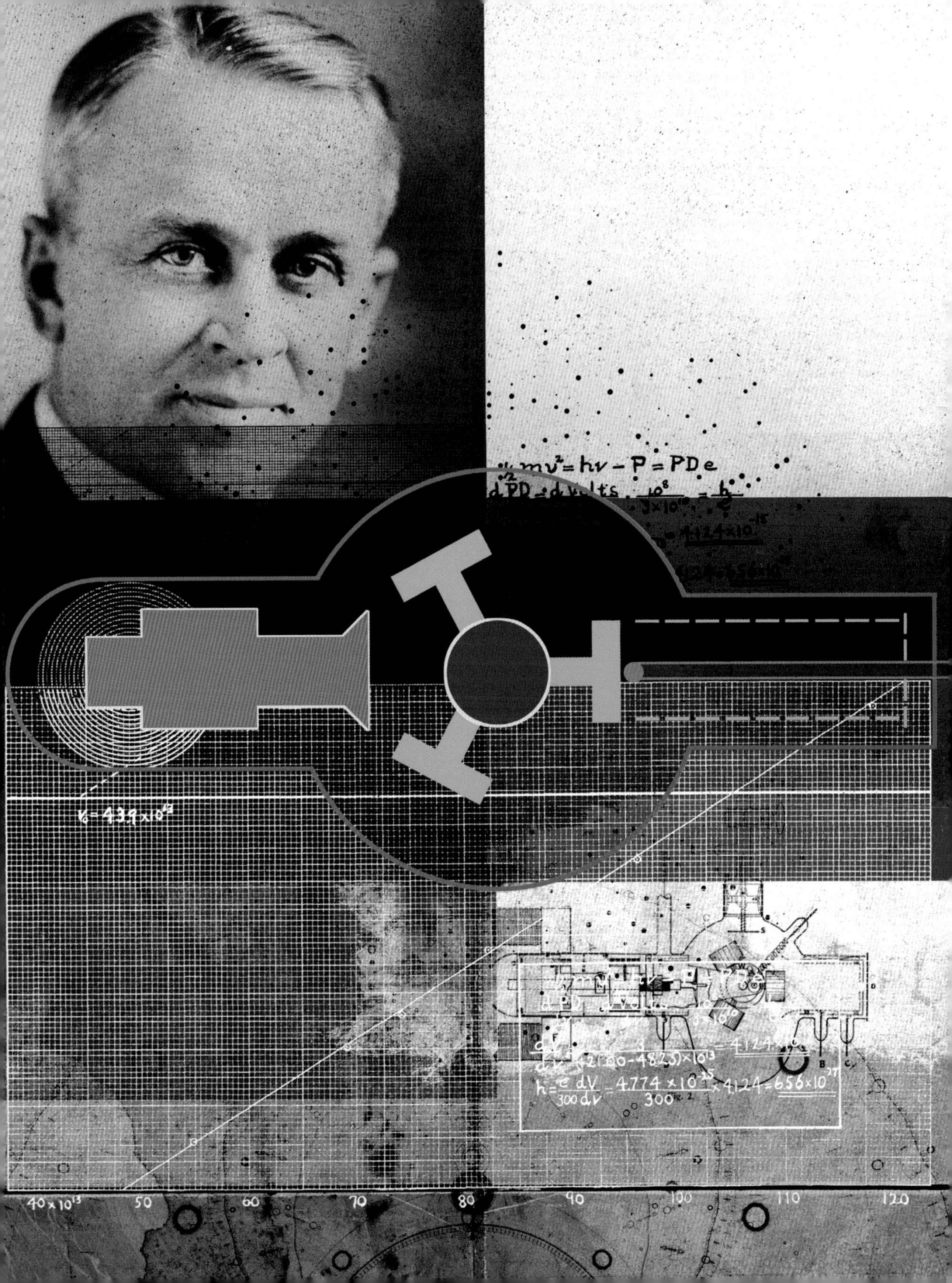
½ mv² = hν − P = PDe
ν₀ = 43.9×10¹³
40×10¹³
50
60
70
80
90
100
110
120

QUANTIZED VIBRATIONS

the 30-second theory

In 1907, Einstein solved a mystery that had been puzzling scientists concerning heat capacity – a measure of the amount of heat needed to increase the temperature of a material. Classical physics predicted that the heat capacity of solids should be constant and should not change with temperature, but experiments suggested that this was not the case and that heat capacity was temperature-related. Einstein realized that this could be due to a quantum effect. He saw that if light were quantized, then it would make sense for heat – which is thermal energy – to be quantized as well. Heat is manifested through the motion of atoms and greater heat means more atomic movement. Atoms in solids have less freedom of movement than atoms in gases and liquids and so exhibit their motion through vibration. Einstein thought of each atom in a solid as an independently vibrating point – or oscillator. He reasoned that if heat is quantized then these vibrations should be quantized, too, making the vibrating material act as if there were a particle passing through it – this 'quasi-particle' obeys quantum theory. This important insight was published in a paper entitled *Die Plancksche Theorie der Strahlung und die Theorie der spezifischen Wärme*. It provided further support for the existence of quanta.

3-SECOND THRASH

Einstein added to evidence for the existence of energy quantization by explaining how quantized atomic vibrations can cause heat capacity to change with temperature.

3-MINUTE THOUGHT

The thermal energy of a group of oscillating atoms bound together in a crystal structure leads to vibrations in the lattice. Heat energy is converted into the mechanical energy of the vibrating lattice, which can transport heat and sound through the material. These vibrations, which act like waves passing through a crystal, have energy and momentum associated with them – and exhibit particle-like properties. A quantum of this vibrating mechanical energy is called a phonon.

RELATED ENTRIES

See also
BOSE-EINSTEIN CONDENSATES
page 28

PHOTOELECTRIC QUANTA
page 36

3-SECOND BIOGRAPHIES

WALTHER NERNST
1864–1941
German physicist who pioneered the study of matter at low temperatures and realized the significance of Einstein's paper on quantized vibrations

PETER DEBYE
1884–1966
Dutch-born physicist who refined Einstein's work to describe atoms vibrating collectively rather than an independently

30-SECOND TEXT

Leon Clifford

Vibrations in solids, whether due to heat or sound, are quantized, acting as if a particle is passing through the material.

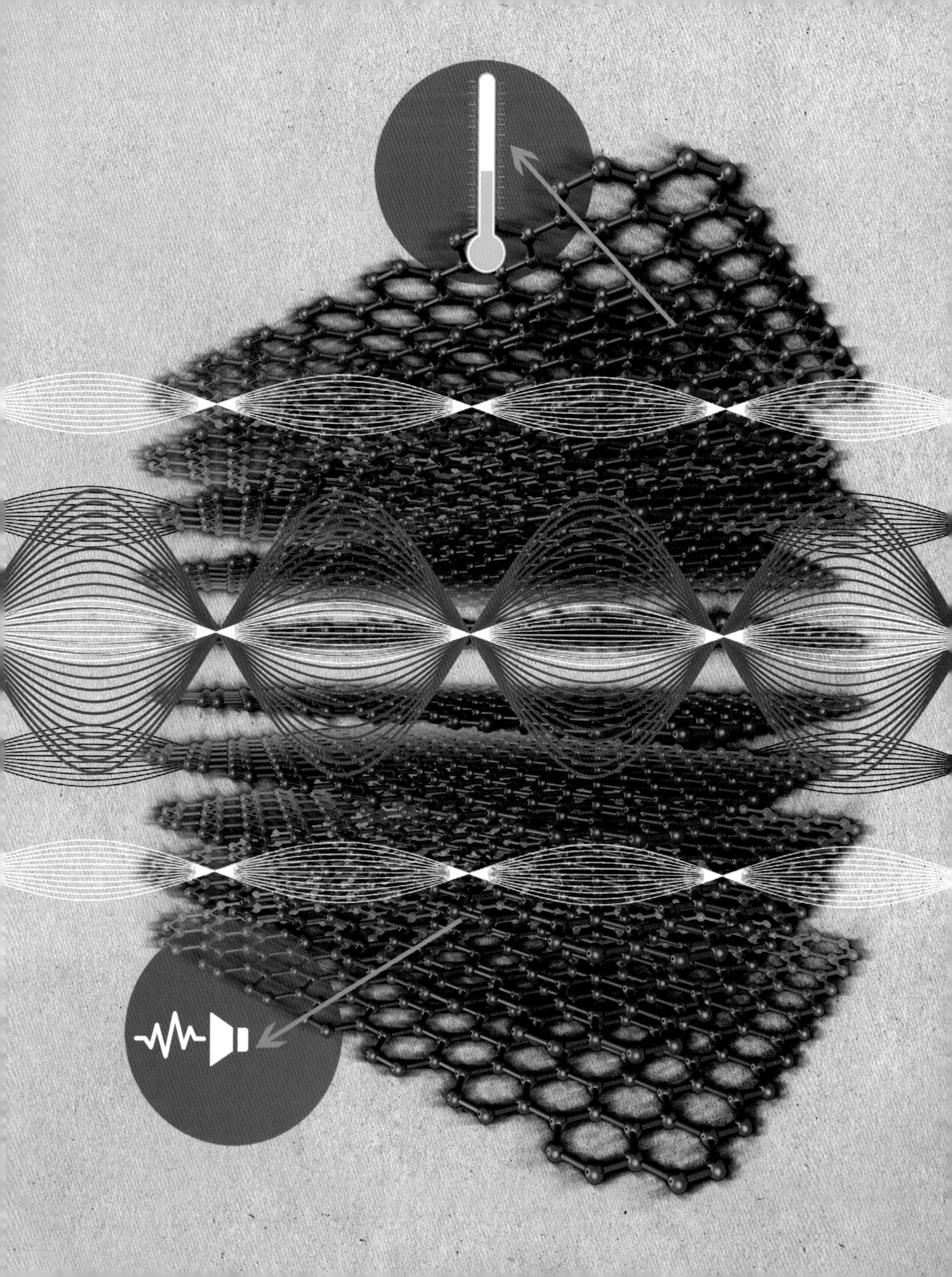

23 April 1858
Born in Kiel, Holstein

1867
Family moves to Munich when his father is appointed professor of law at Munich University

1874
Aged 16, Planck enters the University of Munich to study physics

1877
Spends a year of postgraduate study at the University of Berlin

1879
Completes his PhD in thermodynamics at Munich University

1880
Becomes a *Privatdozent* ('unpaid lecturer') at Munich University

1885
Appointed an extraordinary professor (associate professor) at the University of Kiel

1889
Appointed to succeed Gustav Kirchhoff at the University of Berlin

1892
Promoted to ordinary professor (full professor) of theoretical physics at Berlin

1900
Discovers the 'Planck formula', then later a physical explanation for it, marking the start of the quantum era

1905
Champions Einstein's special theory of relativity, bringing it to the attention of the wider physics community

1914
Signs the 'Manifesto of the 93 Intellectuals' in support of Germany's war effort

1918
Awarded the Nobel Prize in physics for his discovery of 'energy quanta'

1927
Awarded the Lorentz medal

1929
Awarded the Copley medal

1929
The Max Planck medal is inaugurated, the highest award of the German Physical Society

4 October 1947
Dies in Göttingen, aged 89

MAX PLANCK

In 1874, when Karl Ernst Ludwig Marx Planck was entering Munich University to study physics, he was told by one of his professors 'in this field, almost everything is already discovered, and all that remains is to fill a few holes.' Twenty-six years later, the person by then simply known as 'Max' Planck showed how wrong his professor had been by ushering in a new age of physics – the age of the quantum. In order to explain the spectrum of light given off by hot solid bodies (the so-called 'blackbody spectrum'), Planck introduced the idea that energy is quantized. Later in life he would say 'Briefly summarized, what I did can be described as simply an act of desperation.'

Up until 1900 Planck's career had been steady but unremarkable. In 1879 he obtained his PhD from Munich University, writing a dissertation entitled 'On the second law of thermodynamics'. He became a *Privatdozent* ('unpaid lecturer') at Munich, and in 1885 was offered his first paid academic position, as an extraordinary professor (an associate professor) at Kiel University, the city of his birth. Within four years, with the retirement of Gustav Kirchhoff, Planck found himself as an assistant professor at the University of Berlin, and by 1892 he was promoted to full professor. Berlin's first choice had been Ludwig Boltzmann, but he turned the offer down.

Planck continued his theoretical work on thermodynamics, and in 1894 was commissioned by German electric companies to help them develop a better light bulb. Planck wrote his 'Treatise on Thermodynamics' in 1897 and, building on the work of Wilhelm Wien who in 1896 proposed a law to explain the blackbody spectrum, in October 1900 Planck spent an entire night trying to find a mathematical equation that would fit the spectrum, which had by then been fully measured from the ultraviolet to the infrared.

He eventually found an equation, and he shared it with members of the German Physical Society on 19 October 1900. By 13 November, Planck had a theory to explain his equation, but the theory was radical. Planck had to assume that energy was not continuous, but could only come in certain 'chunks', which he called 'quanta'. If he assumed that the quanta tended to zero size, his equation vanished; he was stuck with them. Planck was awarded the Nobel Prize in 1918 for this discovery, but for many years he believed this quantization of energy was not real. He had, in fact, discovered the most important basic idea in physics; that nature is quantized and not continuous. After his death in 1947, the German government named all the government-funded research institutes the 'Max Planck institutes' in his honour.

Rhodri Evans

TOWARDS WAVE-PARTICLE DUALITY

the 30-second theory

The pattern of electromagnetic radiation emitted by a theoretically perfect radiator – a blackbody – puzzled scientists during the 19th century and became known as 'the radiation problem'. In 1900, Max Planck formulated an equation to describe the relationship of the energy of electromagnetic radiation emitted by a blackbody to its frequency – a relationship now known as Planck's Law. Einstein successfully used Planck's approach to explain the mystery of the photoelectric effect. The trouble was that this explanation required physicists to think of light in terms of discrete packets or quanta rather than as waves. In 1909, Einstein tackled this apparent contradiction by assuming Planck's Law was correct and analyzing the terms in the equations describing energy and momentum in blackbody radiation. He showed that one aspect, which dominates at lower energies, is wave-like while another term, which dominates at higher energies, is particle-like. Einstein published these ideas and went on to tell fellow scientists that the apparent contradictions between the wave-like and particle-like behaviour of light 'should not be considered to be non-unifiable'. This was the first articulation of the idea that light can be described both as a wave and as a particle – a concept known as wave-particle duality.

3-SECOND THRASH

Einstein was the first to show that it is not inconsistent or contradictory to think of light as being simultaneously both wave-like and particle-like.

3-MINUTE THOUGHT

Wave-particle duality works both ways. The idea that waves of light can in fact behave like particles of matter was taken a step further in 1924 by French physicist Louis de Broglie. He postulated that particles of matter such as electrons can be described in terms of waves. Electron microscopes make use of this phenomenon by exploiting the way that electrons behave like light waves to illuminate small objects using beams of electrons and then magnify the image.

RELATED ENTRIES

See also
PHOTOELECTRIC QUANTA
page 36

MAX PLANCK
page 42

3-SECOND BIOGRAPHIES

JAMES CLERK MAXWELL
1831–79
Scottish physicist; developed the electromagnetic wave theory of light and radio waves

JAMES HOPWOOD JEANS
1877–1946
English physicist who disagreed with the results of Planck's radiation formula and debated on the nature of light

30-SECOND TEXT

Leon Clifford

Quantum phenomena like light produce effects we expect of waves, like interference where two waves interact – yet also have clear particle-like behaviour.

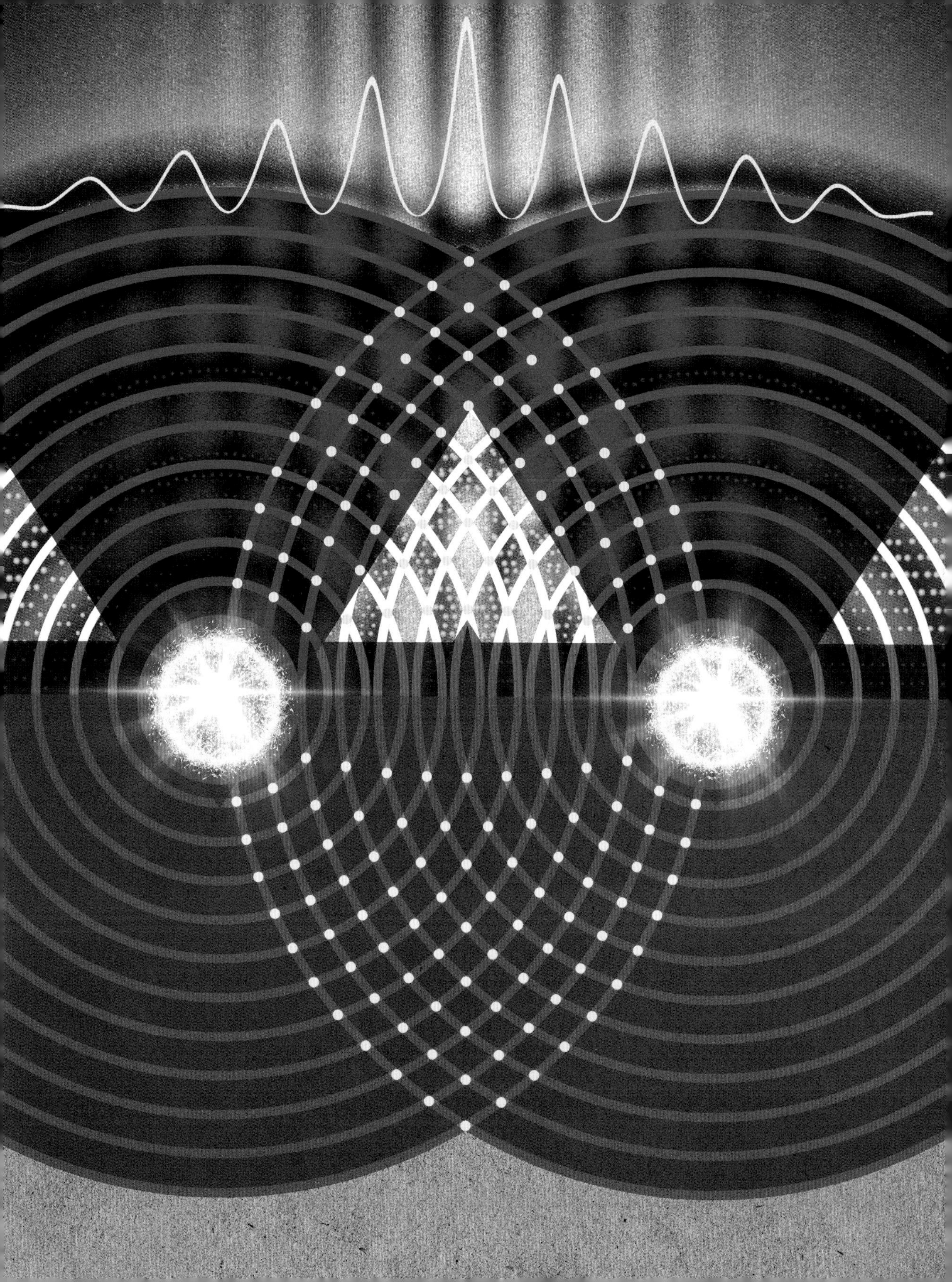

STIMULATED EMISSION

the 30-second theory

Electrons can only inhabit certain orbits around the atomic nucleus, and if they are excited into a higher energy orbit they can return to a lower orbit spontaneously. In returning, the electron emits a particle of light – a photon. Einstein realized that there was an alternative way for an electron to return to a lower orbit – by a process known as stimulated emission. In this process, the electron interacts with an incoming photon that has an energy that corresponds exactly to the energy difference between the orbit in which the electron is and a lower energy orbit. This interaction stimulates the electron to jump down into the lower orbit, and the electron emits a photon whose properties are identical to those of the incoming photon. As these photons pass through the material they can stimulate the production of more and more identical photons. Normally there are more electrons in the lower energy orbits, but by a process called pumping it is possible to put more electrons into the higher energy orbits. This is used in devices such as a laser (Light Amplification by Stimulated Emission of Radiation) to produce an amplified beam of light that has a single frequency and can be focused to a tight spot, allowing a high concentration of energy.

3-SECOND THRASH

In stimulated emission an incoming photon causes an atom to emit a photon with exactly the same properties as the original photon.

3-MINUTE THOUGHT

Lasers are used today in a broad range of everyday applications including CD and DVD players, supermarket barcode scanners, to precisely cut metals and in surgery to correct vision, to clear skin problems and for hair removal. The *Apollo* astronauts placed mirrors on the Moon that allow scientists to monitor the precise distance between it and the Earth by bouncing a powerful laser off the mirrors.

RELATED ENTRIES

See also
PHOTOELECTRIC QUANTA
page 36

QUANTIZED VIBRATIONS
page 40

3-SECOND BIOGRAPHIES

RUDOLF W. LADENBURG
1882–1952
German physicist who was the first person to experimentally confirm Einstein's prediction of stimulated emission

THEODORE H. MAIMAN
1927–2007
American engineer and physicist who was the first person to build a working laser in May 1960

30-SECOND TEXT

Rhodri Evans

An electron can be pushed up to a higher energy level by light, then triggered by another photon to release a pair of photons in stimulated emission.

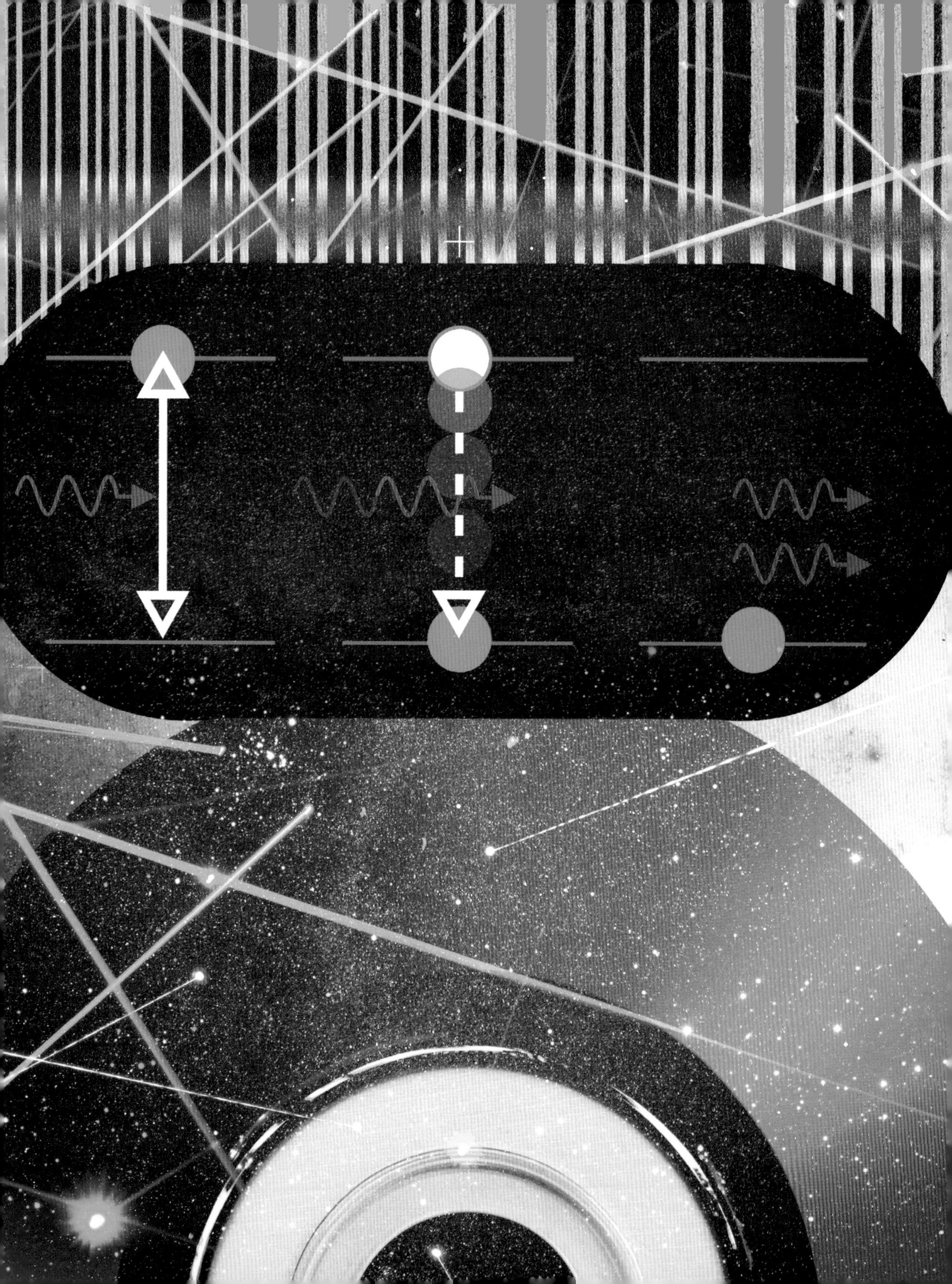

SPECIAL THEORY OF RELATIVITY

SPECIAL THEORY OF RELATIVITY
GLOSSARY

4D Short for 'four dimensional'. We are used to the three dimensions of space – for example up/down, left/right and back/front – each at right angles to the other. Mathematically, there is nothing special about three dimensions and it is possible to have as many dimensions as required. The concept of spacetime made time a fourth dimension, different from the others, but still subject to related mathematics. This made the universe 4D.

gravity In the ancient world, gravity and levity were the tendencies to head towards or away from the centre of the Universe. In English, the term was primarily figurative (referring to something serious and weighty) until the 17th century, when it became more widely used to mean the attractive force felt between two bodies with mass. Einstein redefined gravity in terms of a curvature in spacetime.

Higgs boson Physicists often model the behaviour of matter and other phenomena based on quantum particles as quantum fields. A field is a mathematical description of anything that has a value in each possible space/time location. So, for instance, a weather map showing atmospheric pressure is a two-dimensional pressure field. In this approach, a photon of light becomes a travelling disturbance in the electromagnetic field. When all known fields were combined, it was not enough to explain the mass of some quantum particles. For this reason, a new field was devised, known as the Higgs field after one of its inventors. A travelling disturbance in the Higgs field is called a Higgs boson. The boson doesn't play a major role in the action of the Higgs field, but could be detected, and a particle with a good chance of being a Higgs boson was found in 2013 at CERN, the Europe-wide particle physics laboratory on the French-Swiss border.

Lorentz transformations Dutch physicist Hendrik Lorentz produced a series of equations to handle the results from the Michelson-Morley experiment, showing that light did not seem to be influenced by motion. Physicists speak of an 'inertial frame of reference' – a situation in which time and space can be examined while moving at a steady velocity. The Lorentz transformations produced the changes required to move from one inertial frame to another, resulting in changes in distance and elapsed time as a result of the need to keep the speed of light constant. These transformations are central to special relativity.

Michelson-Morley experiment This experiment, originally conducted in 1887, was to detect the influence of the ether on the speed of light. A circular metal trough, fixed to a brick base, was filled with mercury. On this floated a circular wooden structure with a 1 m (3.3 ft)-wide stone slab on top. Once the slab had been rotated so that it was spinning at a rate of around once every six minutes, it would continue for hours. On top of the slab a series of mirrors relayed a beam of light that was split to travel in right-angled directions before being reunited, where a pattern of fringes would shift if there was any variation in light speed in different directions. The apparatus detected no difference, suggesting that there was no effect on light of the Earth moving through the ether.

spacetime In special relativity it is unrealistic to deal with time or space separately, as movement results in us seeing the passage of time or distances differently. To cope with this, Hermann Minkowski, Einstein's maths lecturer, devised spacetime, a unification of the three dimensions of space and one of time. Interestingly, H. G. Wells had suggested such a unification a little over ten years earlier in his 1895 novella *The Time Machine*.

time dilation Special relativity alters the passage of time, distances and mass for moving objects. The time on a moving object slows when it is observed from a different frame of reference. This slowing of time is referred to as time dilation. The term is derived from the medieval meaning of dilation as delay or procrastination.

FROM PATENTS TO RELATIVITY

the 30-second theory

When Einstein was awarded the position of patent officer (third class) by Swiss patent office director Friedrich Haller, it might not have seemed an ideal post for a high-flying scientist. But the job proved perfect: Einstein found it easy to check the patents, giving him plenty of time for thinking about his own theories. In his 'annus mirabilis' of 1905 he published four major papers, including the one establishing the special theory of relativity. Unexpectedly, some of the patents could have been a direct inspiration for his thinking on simultaneity – the way that two events at separate locations can be considered to happen at the same time, and how being in uniform motion would change the understanding of such simultaneity. This is because the concept of universal time was just becoming accepted and cropped up in some patents. Up to the coming of the railways, each city and town had its own idea of time, setting clocks by sunrise or other natural indications. There could easily be ten or 20 minutes difference between 12 noon in, say, Basel and in Bern. But this was no longer acceptable when trains had to be scheduled, so Einstein dealt with a swathe of patents for the electrical synchronization of clocks.

3-SECOND THRASH
Although Einstein was only a patent office clerk when he developed special relativity, this introduced him to electrically synchronized clocks, a possible inspiration for his ideas on simultaneity.

3-MINUTE THOUGHT
It might seem obvious whether an event, like a clock showing midday, is simultaneous at two locations – but only if we can take a godlike overview. In reality there has to be some way of sending a signal to indicate the time. Before the mid-19th century this was only possible by line-of-sight, but the patents Einstein examined proposed electrical signals to synchronize clocks. Allowing for transmission time, these seemed to mark simultaneous events. But special relativity would throw up issues.

RELATED ENTRIES
See also
DREAMING ABOUT LIGHT
page 54

ON THE ELECTRODYNAMICS OF MOVING BODIES
page 56

SIMULTANEITY
page 62

3-SECOND BIOGRAPHIES
MARCEL GROSSMANN
1878–1936
Friend of Einstein's who lent him his lecture notes and arranged for Einstein's job at the Swiss patent office

FRIEDRICH HALLER
fl. 1888–1921
Director of the Swiss patent office for 33 years and a friend of Marcel Grossmann's father

30-SECOND TEXT
Brian Clegg

The railways brought the need for a universal time, inspiring many patents to synchronize clocks at different stations.

ain - Anzin - Péruwelz
Peruwelz -
INVENTO

DREAMING ABOUT LIGHT

the 30-second theory

When Einstein was only 16 and still in high school in Aarau in Switzerland, he imagined what it would be like to ride alongside a light beam. He later said, 'If a person could run after a light wave with the same speed as light, you would have a wave arrangement which would be completely independent of time. Of course, such a thing is impossible.' Putting this another way, James Clerk Maxwell's equations for electromagnetism predicted that light waves are produced when the electric and magnetic fields for an observer change with time. An observer riding alongside a beam of light would not see the fields changing, and so the light waves would disappear. Maxwell also predicted a unique value for the speed of light, which depended only on the magnetic and electrical properties of empty space. Why should these change if a person were moving? These childhood thoughts culminated ten years later in 1905 in Einstein's paper 'On the Electrodynamics of Moving Bodies', in which he argued that the speed of light was constant for all observers, no matter how quickly they were moving; combining this idea with the existing laws of motion resulted in strange implications for the impact of motion on the nature of time and space.

3-SECOND THRASH

As a 16-year old boy, Einstein wondered what would happen to light if you moved alongside it; conventional wisdom said it would disappear, but he thought this was wrong.

3-MINUTE THOUGHT

The ten-year gap between Einstein dreaming about light and his developing the special theory of relativity was mirrored later when, in 1907, he thought of the principle of equivalence but then took eight years to develop the mathematics of the general theory of relativity. Einstein used thought experiments ('*Gedankenexperiment*' in German) to put forward his ideas; thought experiments are a powerful tool for theoretical physicists.

RELATED ENTRIES

See also
ON THE ELECTRODYNAMICS OF MOVING BODIES
page 56

FAREWELL TO THE ETHER
page 58

3-SECOND BIOGRAPHIES

GALILEO GALILEI
1564–1642
Italian natural philosopher who argued that no mechanical experiment could distinguish between being at rest or moving with a constant velocity – 'Galilean relativity'

JAMES CLERK MAXWELL
1831–79
Scottish theoretical physicist who showed that the speed of light was dependent on the magnetic and electrical properties of space

30-SECOND TEXT

Rhodri Evans

As a teenager Einstein imagined floating alongside a beam of light and observing the light, apparently stopped by his motion.

ON THE ELECTRODYNAMICS OF MOVING BODIES

the 30-second theory

On 30 June 1905 a paper arrived at the offices of *Annalen der Physik* entitled *Zur Elektrodynamik bewegter Körper* from a young patent clerk called Albert Einstein. We now refer to the theory put forward in this landmark paper as the special theory of relativity. This paper, once it was fully digested by the physics community, would overthrow centuries of Newtonian physics and become one of the most important papers in the history of science; it led to our having to change our very concepts of space and time. Based on two postulates – (i) that the speed of light was independent of the motion of the observer and (ii) that the laws of physics would remain the same for any observer moving at a constant velocity – Einstein's paper showed that the long-cherished views that time and space were absolute were incorrect. The paper was published on 26 September 1905, but it would take several years for its importance to be widely recognized. In Germany, one of the physicists who first realized its significance was Max Planck, and through his support Einstein's paper became accepted quite quickly there. In 1907, Einstein's undergraduate mathematics professor introduced the idea of spacetime, and this geometrical interpretation of Einstein's theory led to its wider acceptance.

3-SECOND THRASH

In 1905, Einstein published a paper that showed if we travel near the speed of light time will slow down, lengths will contract and masses will increase.

3-MINUTE THOUGHT

Einstein's special theory of relativity gives rise to the possibility of space travel to distant stars if we can travel quickly enough, because of the effect of time dilation. Additionally, a twin could go on a high-speed journey and return after, say, five years, to find his twin who stayed on Earth has aged by, say, 50 years. At the speed of light itself, time stands still, so a photon travels across the Universe instantaneously from its point of view.

RELATED ENTRIES

See also
FAREWELL TO THE ETHER
page 58

SIMULTANEITY
page 62

LENGTH, TIME & MASS
page 64

3-SECOND BIOGRAPHIES

HENRI POINCARÉ
1854–1912
French mathematician and theoretical physicist who in 1904 came very close to a theory of time dilation

MAX PLANCK
1858–1947
Father of quantum physics, and early champion of Einstein's special theory of relativity

30-SECOND TEXT

Rhodri Evans

In Einstein's breakthrough paper, the fixed speed of light made it impossible to keep an absolute idea of space and time when moving quickly.

FAREWELL TO THE ETHER

the 30-second theory

One of the most contested issues in the genesis of Einstein's 1905 theory of special relativity was the role of the Michelson-Morley experiment. In 1887 Albert Michelson and Edward Morley in Ohio performed an experiment to detect the influence on the speed of light of the ether, the medium in which light waves were thought to move. They measured no difference in speed in two perpendicular directions, contrary to what one would expect as the Earth moves through the stationary ether. This ether stems from an ancient concept: its lineage arguably goes back to the 'fifth element' that, according to Aristotle, filled the heavens, and Isaac Newton postulated an intangible ether that carries light or gravity. In the 19th century the ether was seen as the medium bearing electromagnetic waves, and scientists including Maxwell and Kelvin tried to devise models of it. But Einstein's theory showed that there was no need to invoke a 'luminiferous' (light-bearing) ether at all to understand light's properties. Einstein gave contradictory accounts of whether the Michelson-Morley experiment helped to motivate his theory; his 1905 paper doesn't mention it, and in 1954 he said he wasn't sure if he even knew of it when he developed the theory. Yet there is evidence that he did, and that it stimulated his early thoughts on relativity.

3-SECOND THRASH
Special relativity showed that there was no need to invoke an intangible medium called the ether as the carrier of light waves.

3-MINUTE THOUGHT
Einstein did not, as is commonly said, dispense with the ether; he merely changed it. He regarded some kind of ether-like medium as essential for gravitation; in 1920 he wrote that, 'According to the general theory of relativity space without ether is unthinkable.' But he didn't regard this new ether as a 'ponderable' substance consisting of conventional particles; it was a kind of field. Today such a view of 'ether' is subsumed into the field theories of physics.

RELATED ENTRIES
See also
DREAMING ABOUT LIGHT
page 54

SPACETIME
page 66

3-SECOND BIOGRAPHIES
WILLIAM THOMSON, LORD KELVIN
1824–1907
British scientist who was one of the firmest advocates of the luminiferous ether and suggested that atoms might be vortices in it

EDWARD MORLEY
1838–1923
American scientist who worked on chemistry and optics, and collaborated with Michelson in 1887 to search for the influence of the luminiferous ether

30-SECOND TEXT
Philip Ball

Experiments to measure the speed of light in different directions while moving through the ether showed no evidence of the ether existing.

22 June 1864
Born in Aleksotas in the Russian Empire (now in Lithuania) to German Jewish parents

1872
Family moves to Königsberg in Prussia to escape persecution in Russia

1880
Enters the University of Königsberg

1882–83
Spends the winter semester at the University of Berlin

1883
Awarded the French Academy of Sciences mathematics prize for a paper on the theory of quadratic forms

1885
Obtains his PhD from the University of Königsberg under Ferdinand von Lindemann

1887
Becomes *Privatdozent* (unpaid lecturer) at Bonn University

1892
Appointed extraordinary professor (assistant professor) at Bonn University

1894
Appointed extraordinary professor at the University of Königsberg

1896
Teaches at the ETH in Zurich, where he lectures Einstein in mathematics

1897
Marries Auguste Adler; they would have two daughters together

1902
Appointed ordinary professor (full professor) at Göttingen

1905
Partakes in a seminar on electron theory and discusses ideas of spacetime in relation to Einstein's newly published special theory of relativity

1907
Introduces the concept of spacetime, making Einstein's theory of special relativity far more accessible to non-specialists

12 January 1909
Dies suddenly of appendicitis in Göttingen, German Empire

HERMANN MINKOWSKI

Hermann Minkowski was the third son of Lewin Minkowski and Rachel Taubmann. Born in Russia, his family settled in Königsberg, Germany when Minkowski was eight. His mathematical abilities began to shine at school, where he was spotted by mathematician Heinrich Weber from the town's university. He became interested in quadratic forms – mathematical functions whose variables are squared. We usually encounter quadratic forms with one variable; the equation of a circle is a quadratic form with two variables, x and y, but Minkowski explored quadratic forms with any number of variables.

His doctorate was based on these forms and he went on to win the French Academy of Sciences' Grand Prix for a solution of the ways that an equation with five squares could have an integer solution. In thinking about this, he found he was better able to understand the algebra if he imagined their geometric properties in a multidimensional space. In 1889 he proved a theorem (Minkowski's theorem), which became the foundation of a branch of number theory called the geometry of numbers, and in 1896 he provided a geometric method for solving many problems in number theory – the part of mathematics that deals with natural numbers, integers and prime numbers.

Hermann Minkowski has two key connections to Einstein. First, he lectured the undergraduate Einstein in mathematics in Zurich – he later described him as 'a lazy dog who never bothered about mathematics at all'. After moving to Göttingen, he had a second encounter with Einstein – by now, probably, more appreciative of his former student's abilities. Minkowski had been following the work of Hendrik Lorentz and Einstein, and in 1907 introduced a geometrical portrayal of Einstein's equations of special relativity – the concept of spacetime. With a background in providing a geometric visualization of quadratic forms, Minkowski realized that Einstein's equations of special relativity could be given a geometric portrayal. In 1907 he introduced the idea of four-dimensional spacetime, sometimes known as Minkowski space. In this portrayal, any event has the three dimensions of space (x, y, z) and a fourth dimension of time (t). It enabled the construction of spacetime diagrams, usually showing only one or two of the spatial dimensions for ease of drawing, which provided a way of visualizing the relativity of length, time and simultaneity for different observers.

Minkowski went back to his interest in quadratic forms, and also did original work on the nested 'continued fractions' which have the form $x = 1/(a+(1/b+(1/c+(\dots))))$, though he is most remembered for his work on spacetime and for his more general geometry of numbers. Minkowski died suddenly in 1909 of acute appendicitis. He was only 44 years old.

Rhodri Evans

SIMULTANEITY

the 30-second theory

In special relativity, not only is the passage of time relative, but so is the outcome of measuring whether or not two events are simultaneous. If two events, A and B, occur with no spatial separation between them, then all observers will agree as to which happened first. However, if the two events are separated in space, different observers may disagree as to whether A or B happened first, or whether they were simultaneous. Imagine Anne sitting in the middle of a railway carriage. She simultaneously flashes two lights, one towards the front of the carriage and the other towards the back. At the moment that she makes the flashes, she passes a platform where Brian is standing. For that brief moment, Anne and Brian are in the same place and so both agree that the beams left Anne simultaneously. Anne will also see the beams arrive at the front and back of the carriage simultaneously, but Brian will not. In his frame of reference, the back of the carriage moves towards the light, and the front of the carriage away from it; so from his viewpoint, the back of the carriage receives its flash before the front does. A third person, Charles, travelling faster than the carriage and in the same direction, will think that the front of the carriage receives the light first.

3-SECOND THRASH

If two events A and B do not occur in the same place, whether they happen at the same time depends on the relative motion of the observer to the two events.

3-MINUTE THOUGHT

The relativity of simultaneity calls into question our whole concept of the passage of time. The sequence of two events A and B is no longer absolute, two different observers can disagree as to which event happens first. This has consequences for our perception of what is occurring now and what has occurred in the past.

RELATED ENTRIES

See also
DREAMING ABOUT LIGHT
page 54

ON THE ELECTRODYNAMICS OF MOVING BODIES
page 56

LENGTH, TIME & MASS
page 64

3-SECOND BIOGRAPHIES

HENDRIK LORENTZ
1853–1928
Dutch physicist who derived a mathematical form of the relativity of simultaneity that he called local time

DANIEL COMSTOCK
1883–1970
American physicist and engineer who was the first to suggest a thought experiment to illustrate the relativity of simultaneity

30-SECOND TEXT

Rhodri Evans

Events that appear simultaneous to an observer on a moving train wouldn't be simultaneous to someone on the tracks.

LENGTH, TIME & MASS

the 30-second theory

In Einstein's special theory of relativity, the concept that all observers will agree on their measurements of length and time has to be abandoned. He argued that if two observers, Alice and Brian, are moving relative to each other they will both measure the speed of light to be the same; but as a consequence they will not agree on their measurements of length, time or mass. Instead, they will measure these to be different in the other reference frame compared to their own. These effects are negligible until the relative speed between Alice and Brian is about half the speed of light, and the effects increase as the relative speed approaches the speed of light. If Alice observes Brian's frame of reference, she will measure his 90 cm (3 ft) ruler to be shorter than her own 90 cm ruler, an effect called length contraction. Similarly, she will measure his clock to be ticking more slowly than her own clock, an effect called time dilation. Thirdly, she will think that masses in Brian's frame of reference have increased compared to masses in her own. As special relativity is symmetrical, Brian will think the reverse – that Alice's lengths are shorter and her seconds are longer and masses are greater compared to his. Length, time and mass are all relative.

3-SECOND THRASH

In order for all observers to measure the same speed of light, Einstein had to abandon absolute space and time; near the speed of light lengths get shorter, time is dilated and masses get heavier.

3-MINUTE THOUGHT

Because of time dilation effects (or length contraction – they are just two sides of the same coin), time stands still for a photon travelling at the speed of light, and space shrinks to zero. From its viewpoint, a photon is therefore everywhere in the Universe simultaneously! If we could travel near the speed of light, long-distance space travel would become possible because of time dilation effects.

RELATED ENTRIES

See also
ON THE ELECTRODYNAMICS OF MOVING BODIES
page 56

SIMULTANEITY
page 62

SPACETIME
page 66

3-SECOND BIOGRAPHIES

GEORGE FITZGERALD
1851–1901
Irish physicist who in 1889, came up with the idea of 'length-contraction' to explain the null result of the Michelson-Morley experiment where no motion through the ether was detected

HENDRIK LORENTZ
1853–1928
Dutch physicist who in an attempt to explain the Michelson-Morley experiment, suggested that lengths contract

30-SECOND TEXT

Rhodri Evans

Special relativity made the measurement of time, length and mass dependent on the motion of the observer.

SPACETIME

the 30-second theory

3-SECOND THRASH
Spacetime is a four-dimensional model that helps us graphically visualize the effects of special relativity.

3-MINUTE THOUGHT
The concept of spacetime was central in Einstein's development of general relativity, his theory of gravity. In this theory, the idea of gravity as a force was replaced by the idea that masses warp spacetime: the more massive the object, the more it warps spacetime. This means that, for instance, an orbiting satellite is attempting to travel in a straight line, but the warp in the spacetime it travels through makes it curve.

In special relativity, the equation for the measurement of length in reference frame A depends on the measurements of both length and time in reference frame B. Similarly, the measurement of time in reference frame A depends on the measurements of both length and time in reference frame B. Einstein thus showed that time and space were interlinked. In 1907 Hermann Minkowski developed the idea of spacetime, a four-dimensional model that combines the three dimensions of space and the one dimension of time. One of the advantages of thinking in terms of spacetime is that it allows us to visualize the effects of special relativity. To do this, we usually represent space (x) along the horizontal axis and the speed of light multiplied by time (ct – to also give units of length) along the vertical axis. However, if reference frames A and B are moving relative to each other, their axes will be shifted. To Anne, her x and ct axes will be at right angles to each other, but she will perceive Brian's axes x' and ct' as being shifted as shown in the figure. If an event E happens at some point in space and time, this diagram graphically shows that Anne's measurement of its position (measured horizontally) and its time (measured vertically) will differ from Brian's (measured along x' and ct').

RELATED ENTRIES
See also
HERMANN MINKOWSKI
page 60

LENGTH, TIME & MASS
page 64

A CURVE IN SPACE & TIME
page 118

3-SECOND BIOGRAPHIES
HERMANN MINKOWSKI
1864–1909
Russian mathematician who taught Einstein mathematics and who developed the spacetime concept and diagrams, which initially Einstein did not like

JAMES JEANS
1877–1946
English astrophysicist whose 1947 *The Growth of Physical Science* gave a concise summary of the development of spacetime theory

30-SECOND TEXT
Rhodri Evans

A Minkowski diagram graphically illustrates the relationships in spacetime, a concept that would transform our ideas of gravity.

ct
ct'
A
x'
a
x

EINSTEIN & THE WORLD

EINSTEIN & THE WORLD
GLOSSARY

binding energy The nucleons in an atom stay together despite the repulsion between positively charged protons. This is because nucleons are attracted to each other by the strong nuclear force, which is much stronger than electromagnetism when particles are practically touching. The binding energy of a nucleus is the energy needed to pull its nucleons apart. When light nuclei combine, the resultant combination has a lower overall binding energy, so energy is given off in nuclear fusion. Similarly, when heavy nuclei split into two, the overall binding energy is lower, so energy is produced by nuclear fission.

controlled nuclear reactor The discovery of nuclear chain reactions made the atomic bomb possible, but also opened the way to nuclear reactors in which a controlled process allowed a steady production of heat for electricity generation. In the controlled reactor, sufficient chain reactions are allowed to take place to keep the reaction going, but excess neutrons are absorbed using damping materials called control rods, ensuring that the reaction never runs out of control.

cyclotron Linear accelerators are limited by length – the longest is around 3 km (1.9 miles). However, in the early 1930s experimenters realized that by using a magnetic field to send the accelerating particles into a spiral they could achieve far greater acceleration in a small space. Cyclotrons made many discoveries possible, but were phased out as leading-edge technology in the 1950s by synchrotrons, which keep the accelerated beam on a constant path by synchronizing the field to the speed of the beam. The Large Hadron Collider at CERN on the French/Swiss border is a synchrotron.

electron microscope In quantum physics, the dividing line between particles and waves is non-existent. Phenomena that had been thought of as waves, like light, acted as particles, while particles, like electrons, acted as waves. This is the inspiration for the electron microscope, which uses a beam of electrons in place of the light in a conventional microscope. Microscopes are limited by wavelength; but because the wavelength of electrons is much shorter than that of light, an electron microscope gives far greater magnification.

linear accelerator A piece of apparatus dating back to the 1920s that accelerates electrically charged particles like electrons and protons to high speeds using an oscillating electrical field. By carefully spacing a series of electrodes, the field can be made to accelerate particles repeatedly to extremely high speeds before crashing them into a target. This can be used to produce X-rays or to study new particles produced in the collision.

Manhattan Project Set up in 1942, the Manhattan Project was the top-secret US venture to produce a nuclear fission bomb. Named after the location of the Corps of Engineers office where the undertaking began, the Manhattan Project involved the work of thousands of people across many sites – most famously Los Alamos in New Mexico, where the bombs were developed. Many leading Allied physicists took part in the Manhattan Project, with the notable exception of Albert Einstein.

nucleon A generic term for the particles in the nucleus of an atom: protons and neutrons. Protons are positively charged and neutrons neutrally charged, with very similar masses. The number of protons in the nucleus determines the element, while different possible numbers of neutrons produce the isotopes of the element.

second law of thermodynamics Based on the interaction of the atoms in a material, the 'laws of thermodynamics' were developed to help improve the functioning of steam engines, but became central to understanding energy. The second law states that in a closed system – one in which there is no opportunity for energy to enter or leave – heat will flow from a hotter to a cooler body. This implies that a quantity known as entropy increases, as the law reflects the way that statistically the level of disorder in a body (its entropy) stays the same or increases with time and can only be made to decrease consistently by putting energy into the system.

ON THE ENERGY & INERTIA OF BODIES

the 30-second theory

The fourth of Einstein's great papers, written in 1905 while he was still working at the Swiss patent office, had a typically obscure title. Submitted to *Annalen der Physik* on 27 September and published on 21 November, this short paper, 'Ist die Trägheit eines Körpers von seinem Energieinhalt abhängig?' (Does the inertia of a body depend upon its energy content?), was little more than a page. Building on his original special relativity paper, Einstein deduced with relatively simple mathematics that the kinetic energy of a body diminishes as a result of the emission of light, and the amount that the energy goes down is independent of any properties of the body. Einstein calculated that the reduction in kinetic energy was $\frac{1}{2}xv^2$ where x was E/c^2, E was the energy of the light given off and c the speed of light. Most of us will be familiar from school with the equation $K = \frac{1}{2}mv^2$ deriving the kinetic energy of a moving body from its mass and velocity. So if the kinetic energy reduced by $\frac{1}{2}xv^2$ without the velocity changing, the body had lost x in mass. This loss of mass was the equivalent of E/c^2 in light energy. So the lost mass $m = E/c^2$, which is trivial to rearrange as the more familiar $E=mc^2$, a formula that does not appear in the paper.

3-SECOND THRASH

Einstein's fourth great paper of 1905 used the assumptions of his special relativity paper to show that an emission of light energy should result in a reduction of mass.

3-MINUTE THOUGHT

At the time Einstein wrote the paper, this was a purely theoretical result, though it followed directly from his combination of Maxwell's equations with light always travelling the same speed. But Einstein notes at the end of the paper that it was possible the theory could be put to the test with bodies whose energy content was highly variable (such as radium salts), and that if the theory corresponded to the facts, radiation would carry inertia from one body to another.

RELATED ENTRIES

See also
E=MC²
page 74

MAKING EINSTEIN'S EQUATION A REALITY
page 80

3-SECOND BIOGRAPHIES

MICHELE BESSO
1873–1955
Swiss engineer who worked with Einstein at the Swiss patent office in Bern and whom Einstein said was a sounding board for his 1905 papers

MAURICE SOLOVINE
1875–1958
Romanian mathematician who with Einstein and Conrad Habicht founded a discussion group, Olympia Academy, at which Einstein's 1905 ideas were discussed

30-SECOND TEXT

Brian Clegg

The conversion of mass into energy, according to Einstein's famous equation, provides the power source of a star like the Sun.

m=E/c2
E=mc2

$E=MC^2$

the 30-second theory

$E=mc^2$ is probably the most famous equation in physics. It has even featured in the lyrics of popular songs. The E in the equation is energy, m is the mass and c^2 is the speed of light c multiplied by itself. It is often referred to as mass-energy equivalence and it came to Einstein as an afterthought to his special theory of relativity. It showed that mass and energy are related at a fundamental level. Thus an object has some intrinsic energy even when it is not moving, something we call its rest energy. Because the speed of light is such a large number, even a small mass has a huge amount of energy bound up in it, if only we can release it. When we burn a fossil fuel such as coal, the energy released is due to a change in the chemical bonds in the coal. The carbon in the coal combines with oxygen in the air to produce carbon dioxide; but there is no actual loss of mass in the process. If we actually convert mass to energy, a huge amount of energy can be released. For example, just 1 g of matter contains the energy equivalent of 90 trillion joules, which is equivalent to the energy produced in burning about 3 million kg of coal.

3-SECOND THRASH
The most famous equation in physics states that mass and energy are equivalent; converting mass releases a huge amount of energy.

3-MINUTE THOUGHT
The energy of the Sun is produced by hydrogen fusing to create helium in its core. This is also the principle behind the hydrogen bomb, but performing a controlled fusion reaction currently remains beyond our technical abilities. Achieving such a reaction would allow the hydrogen in water to be used as a fuel, providing essentially unlimited energy from the world's oceans.

RELATED ENTRIES
See also
ON THE ELECTRODYNAMICS OF MOVING BODIES
page 56

ON THE ENERGY & INERTIA OF BODIES
page 72

3-SECOND BIOGRAPHIES
HENRI POINCARÉ
1854–1912
French physicist who saw that if we look at the kinetic energy of an object in two reference frames a paradox arises. He argued that another energy had to exist to get around this

JOHN COCKROFT
1897–1967
British physicist who, with Ernest Walton, conducted the first transmutation experiment that used a proton to split lithium into two helium nuclei

30-SECOND TEXT
Rhodri Evans

The large value of c^2 in the equation means a small amount of matter can produce far more energy than traditional chemical reactions.

FRIDERICVS GVILELMVS III STVDIO ANTIQVITATIS OMNIGENAE ET ARTIVM LIBERALIVM MVSEVM
$E=mc^2$

THE CHAIN

the 30-second theory

3-SECOND THRASH
Nuclear energy can be released in a self-sustaining process in which neutrons released during radioactive decay split other atoms and liberate still more neutrons – and energy.

3-MINUTE THOUGHT
The term 'atomic bomb' was coined by the writer H. G. Wells, who drew on the nuclear work of Rutherford and others to predict them in his 1914 novel *The World Set Free*, which forecast the state of the world to come. Winston Churchill was a fan of the book, and he wrote about atomic bombs in a 1924 article. Leo Szilard read Wells' novel just two years before he worked out how such a bomb might be made.

The phenomenal amount of energy locked up inside the atom became apparent soon after the discovery of radioactivity, before the structure of the atom was fully understood. In 1903 Ernest Rutherford and Frederick Soddy estimated how much energy was being slowly released from atoms that decay radioactively, and Rutherford concluded that if some way could be found to release it all at once, 'some fool in a laboratory might blow up the universe unawares'. Could that be done? A decade or so later it became clear where the energy was coming from: it was the 'binding energy' of the atomic nucleus, produced when a tiny fraction of the mass of the protons and neutrons in the nucleus was converted to energy according to Einstein's iconic equation $E=mc^2$. It could be liberated by 'splitting the atom' – breaking up the nucleus by a collision with some other particle. The neutron, discovered in 1932, was an excellent projectile for doing that. In 1934 Leo Szilard realized that this could be the key to a self-sustaining process of nuclear decay to liberate atomic energy. If there existed an atom that could be split with neutrons but also emitted neutrons in the decay process, you would have a chain reaction. Run it slowly, and you have a source of energy. Let it happen all at once, and you have a bomb.

RELATED ENTRIES
See also
$E=MC^2$
page 74

MAKING EINSTEIN'S EQUATION A REALITY
page 80

THE ROOSEVELT LETTER
page 82

3-SECOND BIOGRAPHIES
ERNEST RUTHERFORD
1871–1937
New Zealand-born physicist whose experiments revealed the structure of the atom and its nucleus

LEO SZILARD
1898–1964
Hungarian-American physicist who first conceived of a nuclear chain reaction in England, and filed a patent for the idea in 1934

30-SECOND TEXT
Philip Ball

In the atomic bomb the energy from a splitting atom is used to split more atoms in a chain reaction producing large quantities of energy.

U
431

11 February 1898
Born in Budapest, Hungary

1917
Joins Austrian Army, cutting short his studies

1919
Moves to Berlin, where he studies physics under Einstein

1922
Earns a doctorate for his work on thermodynamics

1926
Collaborates with Einstein on a new type of refrigerator

1933
Moves to London when Hitler comes to power in Germany

1934
Files a patent on the nuclear chain reaction

1938
Moves to New York, where he works at Columbia University

1939
Drafts the letter to Roosevelt that was signed by Einstein

1942
Moves to Chicago, where he witnesses the first controlled nuclear reaction

1945
Organizes an unsuccessful last-minute petition against dropping the atomic bomb

1948
Shifts his research focus from physics to biology

1963
Becomes a fellow of the Salk Institute for Biological Studies in California

30 May 1964
Dies in La Jolla, California

LEO SZILÁRD

Leo Szilárd was a student, and then a colleague, of Einstein in the 1920s. Over the course of the following decade, Szilárd became one of the first people to recognize the potential of nuclear weapons. He was responsible for drafting the famous letter on the subject that Einstein sent to President Roosevelt in 1939.

Born in Hungary, Szilárd moved to Berlin in 1919 to study physics under Einstein and others. His doctoral thesis, on thermodynamics, was particularly praised by Einstein. After receiving his doctorate in 1922 he remained in Berlin as a research assistant, with his interests gradually shifting towards nuclear theory. His best remembered work of this period, however, was on a much more practical subject – a collaboration with Einstein on a new kind of refrigerator with no moving parts.

Szilárd moved to London in 1933. Shortly afterwards he saw a newspaper article quoting Lord Rutherford as saying the idea of nuclear power was 'moonshine'. Trying to see a way round Rutherford's objections, Szilárd came up with the idea of a nuclear chain reaction and embarked on a search for a practical implementation. It was not until 1939, however, that he saw the way forward. By that time he had moved to Columbia University in New York, and it was there that he first learned about uranium fission. He saw immediately that it could lead to a self-sustaining chain reaction – and potentially the most destructive bomb the world had ever known. The following year he visited Einstein in Princeton and discussed the possibilities with him. The outcome was the famous letter to President Roosevelt – written by Szilárd and signed by Einstein – which led to the setting up of the Manhattan Project and the development of the atomic bomb.

Over the next few years, Szilárd worked with Enrico Fermi – an Italian nuclear physicist who had also recently arrived at Columbia University – on the problem of nuclear fission. The two produced a design for a controlled nuclear reactor, which was successfully tested in December 1942. Nevertheless, Szilárd remained deeply worried about the destructive potential of an atomic bomb. He persuaded 70 prominent scientists to sign a petition urging President Truman not to drop the bomb on Japan. That was in July 1945; the following month the bombs were dropped regardless.

Szilárd was nominated twice for the Nobel Prize, but never received it. After the war, Szilárd's interests turned from physics to biology. He spent his last years as a fellow of the newly formed Salk Institute for Biological Studies in La Jolla, California, where he died of a heart attack in 1964 at the age of 66.

Andrew May

MAKING EINSTEIN'S EQUATION A REALITY

the 30-second theory

The discovery of radioactivity in Paris in 1896 presented a profound puzzle. The rays and particles streaming constantly from a radioactive substance like uranium, no matter what physical state the atoms were in, implied an almost inexhaustible source of energy locked up within the atom itself. It gradually became apparent that this source was the binding energy that holds particles – protons and neutrons, known as nucleons – together in the atomic nucleus. For nuclei heavier than iron, the binding energy per nucleon gets smaller the heavier the nucleus: atomic nuclei can become more stable by shedding nucleons through radioactive decay, or by splitting in nuclear fission. For nuclei lighter than iron, this binding energy per nucleon increases as the atoms get heavier, and so nuclei can gain stability by fusing together. Both nuclear fission of heavy atoms (like uranium) and nuclear fusion of light atoms (like hydrogen) therefore release energy. The products of these processes are a tiny bit lighter than the initial total mass of nucleons, and that mass difference is equivalent to the energy released, via Einstein's $E=mc^2$. This energy is released through fission in nuclear reactors and the first nuclear bombs. Fusion generates relatively more energy, as in thermonuclear 'hydrogen bombs' and the fusion of hydrogen to helium and other elements in stars.

3-SECOND THRASH

Fission and fusion are nuclear reactions that split or combine atomic nuclei, resulting in a very slight mass loss that is converted to energy via $E=mc^2$.

3-MINUTE THOUGHT

Although $E=mc^2$ supplies a useful way to calculate the energy released in nuclear reactions, it was never the immediate inspiration for atom bombs. Early experiments made it clear how much energy could be released by splitting or fusing atoms, and the discovery in 1939 of a chain reaction that could liberate this energy spontaneously would surely have happened regardless of whether Einstein's equivalence of mass and energy was already understood. Einstein was never the 'father of the bomb'.

RELATED ENTRIES

See also
ON THE ELECTRODYNAMICS OF MOVING BODIES
page 56

THE CHAIN
page 76

THE ROOSEVELT LETTER
page 82

3-SECOND BIOGRAPHIES

LISE MEITNER
1878–1968
Austrian physicist who, with Otto Frisch, first explained the experimental discovery of uranium fission in terms of a splitting of the nucleus

ENRICO FERMI
1901–54
Italian physicist who built the first working nuclear fission reactor ('pile') in Chicago in 1942

30-SECOND TEXT

Philip Ball

In a fission reactor, a nuclear fission chain reaction is controlled to produce a steady flow of energy to heat water and produce electricity.

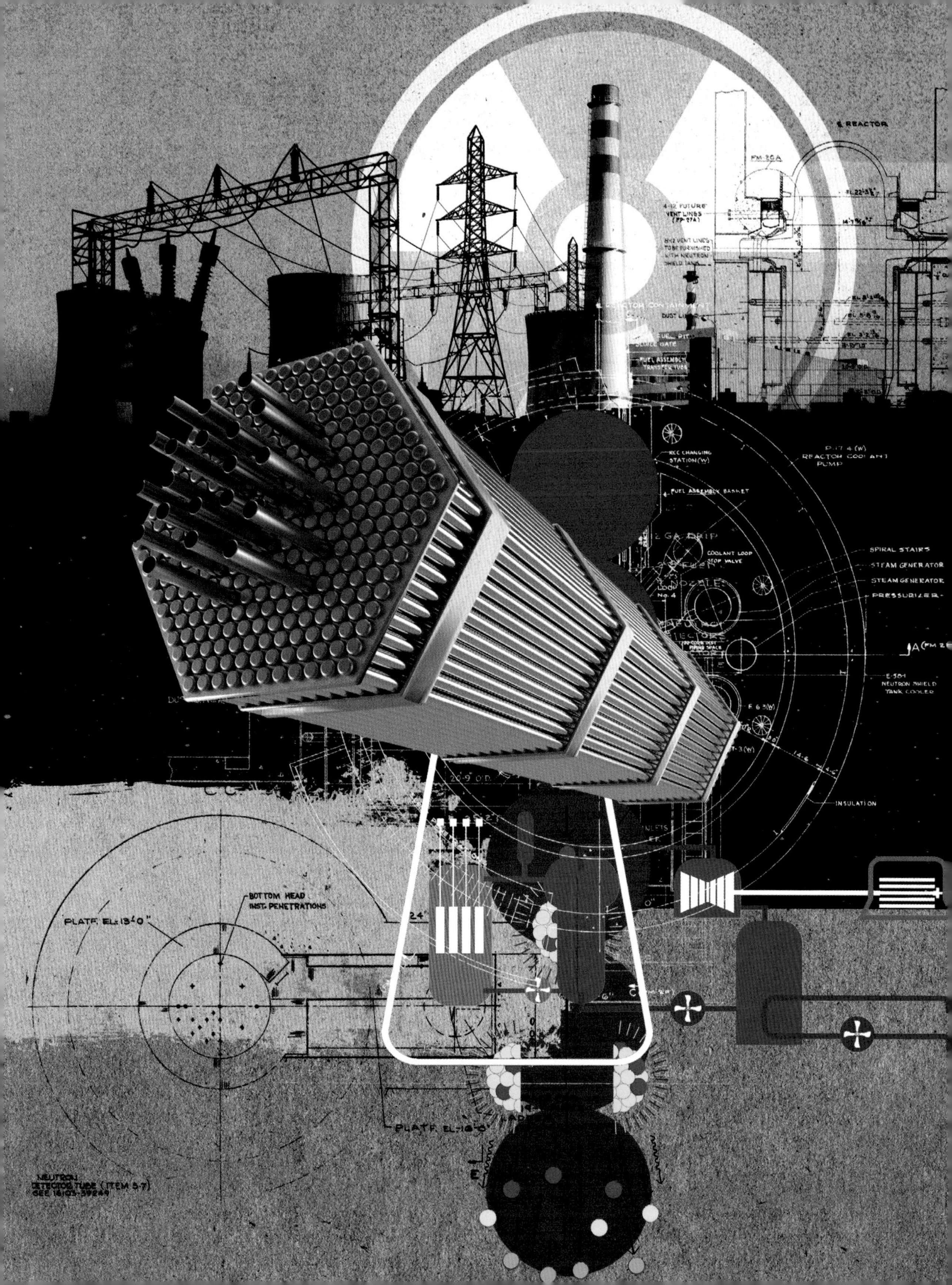
REACTOR
FM-30A
4-12 FUTURE VENT LINES (FP-27A)
REACTOR CONTAINMENT
DUST LINER
FUEL PIT
SLUICE GATE
FUEL ASSEMBLY TRANSFER TUBE
REACTOR COOLANT PUMP
STATION (W)
FUEL ASSEMBLY BASKET
COOLANT LOOP STOP VALVE
SPIRAL STAIRS
STEAM GENERATOR
STEAM GENERATOR
PRESSURIZER
NEUTRON SHIELD TANK COOLER
INSULATION
BOTTOM HEAD INST. PENETRATIONS
PLATF. EL. 13'-0"
PLATF. EL. 13'-0"
NEUTRON DETECTOR TUBE (ITEM 5-7)

THE ROOSEVELT LETTER

the 30-second theory

3-SECOND THRASH
Einstein put his signature to a letter, written by Leo Szilárd, alerting the president of the United States to the potential of atomic weapons.

3-MINUTE THOUGHT
The immediate result of Einstein's letter was the creation of an Advisory Committee on Uranium in October 1939. In less than three years this had evolved into the massive – and ultra-secret – Manhattan Project, which led to the construction of the first atomic weapons. Einstein was never invited to participate in this, because the FBI considered him a security risk. In any case, his pacifist beliefs would probably have led him to refuse any involvement.

When Einstein's friend Leo Szilárd heard about the discovery of uranium fission in 1938 he realized that – coupled with his own concept of a nuclear chain reaction – it pointed the way towards a new kind of super-destructive weapon. His immediate fear was that the Nazis would develop such a weapon, and his top priority was to cut off their access to uranium ore. A major source of this was in Belgian-controlled territories in Africa, which were in danger of being overrun by the Germans. Knowing that Einstein was on friendly terms with the Belgian royal family, Szilárd approached him for assistance. Einstein was horrified at the thought of an atomic bomb – something that had never occurred to him – and agreed to help in any way he could. They decided to bypass the Belgians and go straight to the top of the US administration – warning not just of the Nazi threat, but the need to establish a proactive research programme. The result was a two-page letter – drafted by Szilárd but signed by Einstein – that was delivered to President Roosevelt on 2 August 1939. The letter set wheels in motion that eventually led to the dropping of atomic bombs on Hiroshima and Nagasaki six years later.

RELATED ENTRIES
See also
THE CHAIN
page 76

A VOICE FOR PEACE
page 84

3-SECOND BIOGRAPHIES
FRANKLIN D. ROOSEVELT
1882–1945
The 32nd president of the United States, from March 1933 until his death on 12 April 1945

LEO SZILÁRD
1898–1964
Hungarian-born physicist who settled in the United States in 1938. He was the first person to put forward the idea of a nuclear chain reaction, in 1933

30-SECOND TEXT
Andrew May

US president Franklin Delano Roosevelt was spurred by the letter signed by Einstein to set up the project to produce a nuclear weapon.

Albert Einstein
Old Grove Rd.
Nassau Point
Peconic, Long Island

August 2nd, 1939

F.D. Roosevelt,
President of the [illegible] States,
White House
Washington, D.C.

Sir:

Some recent work by [illegible] Fermi and L. Szilard, which has been communicated to me in manuscript, leads me to expect that the element uranium may be turned [illegible] a new and important source of energy in the immediate [illegible]. Certain aspects of the situation which has arisen seem to call for [illegible] and, if necessary, quick action on the part of the Administration. [illegible] believe therefore that it is my duty to bring to your attention the following facts and recommendations:

In the course of the [illegible] it has been made probable - through the work of [illegible] in France as well as [illegible] and Szilard in America - that it may become possible to set up a nuclear chain reaction in a large mass of uranium, by which vast amounts of power and large quantities of new radium-like elements would be [illegible]. [illegible] almost certain that this could be achieved [illegible].

This new phenomenon would also lead to the construction of bombs, and it is conceivable - though much less certain - that extremely powerful bombs of a new type may thus be constructed. A single bomb of this type, carried [illegible] boat and exploded in a port, might very well destroy the whole port together with some of the surrounding territory. However, such bombs might very well prove to be too heavy for transportation by air.

-2-

The United States has [illegible] poor ores of uranium in moderate quantities. There is some [illegible] Canada and the former Czechoslovakia, while the most important [illegible] Belgian Congo.

In view of this situation [illegible] may think it desirable to have some permanent contact maintained between the Administration and the group of physicists working on chain reactions in America. One possible way of achieving this might be for you to entrust with this task a person who has your confidence and who could perhaps serve in an inofficial capacity. His task might comprise the following:

a) to approach Government Departments, keep them informed of the further development, and put forward recommendations for Government action, giving particular attention to the problem of securing a supply of uranium ore for the United States;

b) to speed up the experimental work, which is at present being carried on within the limits of the budgets of University laboratories, by providing funds, if such funds be required, through his contacts with private persons who are willing to make contributions for this cause, and perhaps also by obtaining the co-operation of industrial laboratories which have the necessary equipment.

I understand that Germany has actually stopped the sale of uranium from the Czechoslovakian mines which she has taken over. That she should have taken such early action might perhaps be understood on the ground that the son of the German Under-Secretary of State, von Weizsäcker, is attached to the Kaiser-Wilhelm-Institut in Berlin where some of the American work on uranium is now being repeated.

Yours very truly,

A. Einstein

(Albert Einstein)

A VOICE FOR PEACE

the 30-second theory

In October 1914, just two months after the outbreak of the First World War, 93 German academics – including Max Planck – issued a robustly militaristic statement supporting Germany's role in the war. Horrified by this 'Manifesto of the 93', Einstein – already a committed pacifist – countered with his own 'Manifesto to Europeans', calling for an immediate end to the conflict. It was a flop, gaining just four signatures, but Einstein had found a new calling: he remained an outspoken voice for peace for the rest of his life. He advocated total disarmament, and encouraged people of all nations to refuse to fight for their country. In a speech in New York City in 1930, he suggested that if just 2 per cent of people refused military service, governments would be forced to call off their plans for war. The idea caught on, and pacifists across America started wearing lapel badges saying '2 per cent'. Following the development of the atom bomb, in which Einstein himself had played a small if unintentional role, his calls for disarmament became even more urgent. One of his final acts, just a week before his death, was to sign the Russell-Einstein Manifesto – produced jointly with the philosopher Bertrand Russell – emphasizing the dangers of nuclear weapons and calling for world peace.

3-SECOND THRASH

Einstein was an outspoken pacifist, advocating disarmament, supporting people who refused military service and drawing attention to the dangers of nuclear warfare.

3-MINUTE THOUGHT

The only time that Einstein's pacifism wavered was when Hitler came to power in 1933, and Germany began to pose a military threat to neighbouring nations such as Belgium. To the amazement of commentators, Einstein changed his tune – advocating military readiness as the only viable response to Nazi aggression. As a headline in the *New York Times* put it: 'Einstein alters his pacifist views: advises Belgians to arm themselves against the threat of Germany.'

RELATED ENTRY

See also
THE ROOSEVELT LETTER
page 82

3-SECOND BIOGRAPHY

BERTRAND RUSSELL
1872–1970
British philosopher and pacifist, who was imprisoned during the First World War for refusing military service

30-SECOND TEXT

Andrew May

For most of his life Einstein supported peace and after the Second World War joined the call for worldwide nuclear disarmament .

F.D. Roosevelt,
the United States,
Washington, D.C.
Sir:
Some recent work by
municated to me in m
ium may be turned int
mediate future. Cert
to call for watc
of the Administr
-2-
quantities.
while the most important
the former Czechoslovakia,
is Belgian Congo.
In view of this situa
think it desirable to have some
and the group
One possible way
of achievin
with this task a person
who has your confidence
capacity. His task might comprise
a) to approach Government De
informed of the
and put forward recommendations for Government action,
particu
to the problem of securing a supply of uran-
for the United States;
Laboratories, by
perhaps also by obtain
the co-operation of industrial laboratories
the necessary e
that Germany has actually stopped the sale of uranium
which she has taken over. That she should
taken such
might perhaps be understood on the ground
the son of the
Under-Secretary of State, von Weizsäcker, is
to the
-Wilhelm-Institut in Berlin where some of the
uranium is now being repeated.
Yours very truly,
(Albert Einstein)
PEACE
UN
HANDU
THE

EINSTEIN'S PATENT

the 30-second theory

We think of Einstein as unworldly and theoretical, but his time in the Swiss patent office wasn't his only experience of inventions. Einstein was the joint author of a successful patent for a refrigerator with fellow physicist Leo Szilárd. Fridges work by making use of the cooling effect of evaporation – just as skin cools when sweat evaporates. In the early days of fridges, the substance pumped around (the refrigerant) was toxic, making leaks dangerous and resulting in the death of a Berlin family in the 1920s. This tragedy inspired Einstein and Szilárd to devise an alternative mechanism with no moving parts, operated at a constant pressure and without the high compression required by a traditional fridge – so far less likely to leak dangerous substances. Although the fridge received many patents (US patent 1781541A, for instance), it was never widely used. But the technology could still be employed: it only requires a source of heat to run, so is ideal for situations with poor or intermittent electricity supplies. Where a conventional fridge uses a compressor, the Einstein/ Szilárd fridge has as its refrigerant a mix of two compounds, one of which can be easily and quickly extracted from the mix. The result is a sudden drop in pressure, providing rapid evaporation and cooling.

3-SECOND THRASH

Einstein is known for the most theoretical of physics, but in 1926, along with fellow physicist Leo Szilárd he invented a new type of refrigerator.

3-MINUTE THOUGHT

Fridges seem to break a fundamental law of physics, the second law of thermodynamics, which says that heat always flows from a hotter to a colder body. In a fridge, heat travels from the cool inside to the warmer outside. However, there is an escape clause in the second law, as it only applies to a closed system. Because energy comes into the fridge from the outside, it is able to pump heat out without breaking the law.

RELATED ENTRIES

See also
ADVENTURES IN STATISTICAL MECHANICS
page 18

FROM PATENTS TO RELATIVITY
page 52

3-SECOND BIOGRAPHIES

LEO SZILÁRD
1898–1964
Hungarian physicist who moved to Germany in 1919, becoming a German citizen. A great technical inventor, Szilárd independently devised the linear accelerator, the cyclotron and the electron microscope as well as the refrigerator concept he developed with Einstein

30-SECOND TEXT

Brian Clegg

In a refrigerator jointly designed with Leo Szilárd, Einstein made his personal contribution to the patents he had once checked.

36
37
27
28
INVENTORS
BY
ATTORNEY

FIGHTING THE QUANTUM

FIGHTING THE QUANTUM
GLOSSARY

CERN In 1952 a Europe-wide particle physics laboratory was planned on the border between France and Switzerland, near Geneva. This was for the European Council for Nuclear Research, or, in French, Conseil Européen pour la Recherche Nucléaire, abbreviated to CERN. By the time the facility opened in 1954 it was renamed the European Organization for Nuclear Research, but OERN is hard to pronounce, so the popular name remained CERN. The laboratory houses a range of major experiments, notably the Large Hadron Collider, and is famous as the birthplace of the World Wide Web.

decoherence Quantum particles can be in a superposition of states. So, for instance, a particle's quantum spin can be in a superposition of states with no actual value, just the probabilities of it being up or down. However, objects made of quantum particles behave 'classically' – as we would expect them to do in line with traditional physics. This classical behaviour is explained by decoherence: the process by which a quantum particle interacting with its environment loses its individual quantum behaviour.

entanglement In 1935, Einstein and a pair of colleagues produced a paper to cast doubt on the reality of quantum physics by showing a result so strange that it seemed impossible: this result was named 'quantum entanglement' by Austrian physicist Erwin Schrödinger. Entanglement says it is possible to place two quantum particles in a state where a change to one particle is immediately reflected in the other, however far they are separated.

hidden variable When particles are entangled, if we make a measurement of, say, the spin of one of the particles and find it to be down, the other must be up. But before measurement, both particles were in a superposition of states – each was *both* up and down. Compare this with a situation in which we have a pair of different coloured socks. If we separate the socks and look at one, we instantly know the colour of the other. But they aren't entangled; the information was already in the system, but hidden away. Einstein suggested that the same applied in quantum physics – that values such as the spin direction were fixed before the entangled particles were separated, but were hidden variables. Experiments since have shown no evidence for hidden variables.

photon Quantum physics emerged from the observation that light is emitted in 'packets' of energy called quanta. As the concept of quanta became applied to a range of quantum entities, the name 'photon' was devised for a light quantum. The word had already been used as a unit of retinal illumination, but American chemist Gilbert Lewis proposed it for the quantum of light in *Nature* in 1926.

quantum weirdness Not an official term, but reflective of the nature of quantum physics. Paradoxically, quantum particles behave entirely differently to the everyday 'macro' objects that we are familiar with, even though those larger objects are made of quantum particles.

Schrödinger's wave equation A wave equation is a mathematical formula describing the way that a wave changes over time. Schrödinger's equation describes how the probabilities of finding a particle in a particular location change with time.

Solvay Conference Belgian businessman Ernest Solvay funded a series of conferences on physics and chemistry. Einstein attended the first physics conference in 1911 and several of the following events, notably the fifth in 1927 on electrons and photons, with a roll call including Bohr, Born, de Broglie, Dirac, Heisenberg, Pauli, Planck and Schrödinger, all formidable names in quantum physics. The conferences continue to this day.

uncertainty principle The principle, devised by Heisenberg, states that there are certain properties of a quantum particle that are linked so that the more accurately one is known, the less we know about the other. The best-known pairing is the position and the momentum of a particle. This is a fundamental behaviour of quantum particles.

LETTERS TO BORN

the 30-second theory

Between 1916 and 1955, Albert Einstein and his friend Max Born exchanged a long sequence of letters in which they discussed the science of the day alongside politics and society. Before this, Einstein had been largely supportive of quantum theory, contributing a number of fundamental concepts. However, by the time he and Born began their correspondence, Einstein was feeling doubt, and as the years went on he increasingly expressed this, including some of his most famous comments. Writing of quantum entanglement: 'I cannot seriously believe in [quantum theory] because the theory cannot be reconciled with the idea that physics should represent a reality in time and space, free from spooky actions at a distance.' Appalled by the randomness at the heart of quantum theory: 'I find the idea quite intolerable that an electron exposed to radiation should choose of its own free will, not only its moment to jump off, but also its direction. In that case, I would rather be a cobbler, or even an employee in a gaming house, than a physicist.' And, most famously, he told Born, 'Quantum theory says a lot, but does not really bring us any closer to the secret of the "old one". I, at any rate, am convinced that He is not playing at dice.'

3-SECOND THRASH
Einstein exchanged many letters over a 40-year period with quantum physicist Max Born, in which he put forward his famous critiques of quantum theory and its use of probability.

3-MINUTE THOUGHT
Born was inevitably the target of Einstein's complaints about quantum physics, not just because Born worked in the area, but also because he was responsible for the interpretation of Schrödinger's wave equation that showed it predicted the probability of finding a particle in a particular location. It was Born who embedded probability in the quantum world, implying that before measurement, a quantum particle had no location, but was simply a collection of probabilities, a concept that appalled Einstein.

RELATED ENTRIES
See also
HIDDEN VARIABLES
page 98

EPR
page 102

ENTANGLEMENT TRIUMPHS
page 104

3-SECOND BIOGRAPHIES
MAX BORN
1882–1970
German physicist who was a major contributor to the development of quantum theory, for which he won the Nobel Prize in physics in 1954

30-SECOND TEXT
Brian Clegg

In letters to his friend Max Born, Einstein complained of the randomness implied by quantum theory and said, if true, he would rather be a cobbler.

29302
AIR MAIL
4c
UNITED STATES
THOMAS JEFFERSON
UNITED STATES
CASINO
4940

EINSTEIN'S SLIT

the 30-second theory

Although Einstein was one of the founders of quantum theory he became increasingly doubtful about the way it seemed to require reality to be based on probabilities, rather than fixed, if unknown, values. Over the years he teased fellow physicist and quantum theorist Niels Bohr with thought experiments designed to show errors in quantum theory. At the fifth Solvay Conference in Brussels in 1927, dedicated to electrons and photons, Einstein conjured up a thought experiment that he believed uncovered a problem with quantum physics. He imagined firing a beam of electrons at a slit, where, with wave-like behaviour, they would diffract, spreading out to hit a curved screen behind the slit at different locations. According to quantum theory, until one spot on the screen lit up for a particular electron, that electron could be anywhere on the screen, with the probability decided by Schrödinger's wave equation. However, Einstein argued, if this were the case, there had to be an instant communication from the spot that lit up to the rest of the screen at the moment the electron arrived. Such instant communication was not allowed by special relativity. Bohr was not impressed and was swift to dismiss the argument.

3-SECOND THRASH

Einstein tried to show that quantum theory was flawed with a thought experiment in which an electron's ability to be in 'more than one place' would require instant communication.

3-MINUTE THOUGHT

Bohr struggled with Einstein's argument, saying 'I feel myself in a very difficult position because I don't understand what precisely is the point which Einstein wants to [make]. No doubt it is my fault.' For Bohr there was no issue because the electron only existed as a set of probabilities until one position was made actual. There was no need to tell other parts of the screen not to glow because only probabilities were present.

RELATED ENTRIES

See also
LETTERS TO BORN
page 92

WEIGHING THE PHOTON
page 96

EPR
page 102

3-SECOND BIOGRAPHIES

NIELS BOHR
1885–1962
Danish physicist who developed the first modern atomic structure and led the development of quantum physics, for which he received the Nobel Prize in 1922

30-SECOND TEXT

Brian Clegg

In a thought experiment at a Solvay Conference, Einstein suggested interfering particles would have to communicate faster than light.

P
O
S
e

WEIGHING THE PHOTON

the 30-second theory

Einstein and Bohr met up at the sixth Solvay Conference in 1930. The conference was on magnetism, but Einstein had spent some time coming up with a challenge to quantum theory for Bohr, and took the opportunity to present it over breakfast. In his thought experiment, he described a box containing a source of radiation, with a shutter-covered hole in the box's side. The shutter was opened for a very short time, during which a single photon flew out. Einstein weighed the box before and after the photon was produced, giving an exact figure for the change in mass corresponding to the photon's energy. And he could measure the timing of the shutter with great accuracy. But one of quantum theory's fundamental features was the uncertainty principle, which says that the more you know about the energy of a particle, the less you can know about exact timing. You shouldn't be able to know both accurately. Bohr was initially baffled. An observer described Einstein walking quietly away from their meeting with a 'somewhat ironical smile' while Bohr trotted excitedly alongside. But by next morning, Bohr had seen the flaw in Einstein's challenge and demolished it.

3-SECOND THRASH
In a second challenge to quantum theory, Einstein presented Bohr with a thought experiment that he thought disproved the uncertainty principle, but Bohr was able to find the experiment's flaw.

3-MINUTE THOUGHT
To uncover Einstein's error, Bohr imagined a specific arrangement of the experiment where the box hangs from a spring, which provides the weight measurement. When the photon is released, the box moves up slightly in response to the change in mass. Bohr then used a result from Einstein's general relativity that showed that moving clocks run slowly, combined with the uncertainty in the rate of movement to establish there would still be the correct uncertainty in energy and time.

RELATED ENTRIES
See also
LETTERS TO BORN
page 92

EINSTEIN'S SLIT
page 94

EPR
page 102

3-SECOND BIOGRAPHIES
ERNEST SOLVAY
1838–1922
Belgian industrialist who funded a series of landmark conferences in physics

NIELS BOHR
1885–1962
Danish physicist and friend of Einstein with whom Einstein kept up a friendly argument on the validity of quantum theory for many years

30-SECOND TEXT
Brian Clegg

Another of Einstein's Solvay challenges to Niels Bohr involved the effect of a departing photon of light on the weight of a box.

Δt

HIDDEN VARIABLES

the 30-second theory

If you toss a fair coin (one that has not been tampered with) and hold it in your hand without looking at it, you would expect a 50 per cent chance the coin is heads and a 50 per cent chance that the coin is tails. However, this isn't strictly true. There was a 50:50 chance before the coin was tossed. But now that the toss has occurred, there is a 100 per cent chance that it is showing whatever value is facing upwards and a 0 per cent chance of the other face. You just don't know what that face is. This kind of information is called a 'hidden variable'. The information is in the system, but it is not possible to access it. Even though probability gives the tools to deduce all kinds of interesting things about what might happen with coin tosses, the coins themselves are never in a probabilistic state. However, a quantum equivalent of a coin is considered to literally only exist as probabilities before examination. Einstein could not accept this and believed that somewhere under the probabilities there was a fixed reality, but there was no way to discover the values.

3-SECOND THRASH
Some apparently probabilistic outcomes, like a coin toss, have 'hidden variables' where the result is fixed before it is revealed, but in quantum theory there are no hidden variables.

3-MINUTE THOUGHT
Physicist John Bell came up with a picture of hidden variables called 'Dr Bertlmann's socks'. His colleague Reinhold Bertlmann always wore odd socks. Bell pointed out that if one of Dr Bertlmann's socks appeared around the corner of a building before you saw the rest of him, and the sock was pink, you would know that the other sock was not pink even though you hadn't seen it. The socks, unlike quantum particles, have hidden variables.

RELATED ENTRIES
See also
LETTERS TO BORN
page 92

EPR
page 102

REALISM & REALITY
page 106

3-SECOND BIOGRAPHIES
JOHN BELL
1928–90
Northern Irish physicist working at CERN who devised a test to demonstrate if hidden variables existed

REINHOLD BERTLMANN
1945–
Austrian physicist who was a close collaborator with John Bell at CERN

30-SECOND TEXT
Brian Clegg

Einstein suggested that, like a tossed coin that has yet to be revealed, quantum particles had hidden values for their state that were revealed when measured.

LIBERTY
IN GOD
WE TRUST
ES OF AMERICA
NUM
DIME

7 October 1885
Born in Copenhagen, son of professor of physiology Christian and his wife Ellen

1911
Awarded his doctorate at Copenhagen University

1911–12
Year spent in England at Cambridge and Manchester sets him on the path to the quantum atom

1913
'Bohr atom' model published

1914
Lectureship in Physics at Manchester University

1916
Becomes professor of theoretical physics at Copenhagen University

1920
Appointed head of the new Institute of Theoretical Physics, Copenhagen University

1922
Receives Nobel Prize in physics for his atomic structure

1927
Fifth Solvay Conference, where Einstein challenges Bohr on quantum theory

1935
Einstein's EPR paper presents a challenge to Bohr

1943
Escapes arrest by German police by crossing to Sweden, subsequently to the UK and then the United States

18 November 1962
Dies in Copenhagen

1965
Danish Institute of Theoretical Physics renamed Niels Bohr Institute

1997
Element 107 named bohrium

NIELS BOHR

In a 2013 'top ten' of physicists in the *Observer* newspaper, Niels Bohr came a surprising second, ahead of Einstein and Galileo. While this position is disputable, there is no doubt that Bohr was central to the development of quantum theory, the physics that describes the behaviour of atoms, electrons and photons. And in this role he was often in friendly dispute with Einstein. After gaining a doctorate in Copenhagen, the young Bohr moved to the UK for a year where he worked with the discoverer of the electron, J. J. Thomson and, far more successfully, with the ebullient Ernest Rutherford in Manchester where Rutherford's team had discovered the atomic nucleus. This led to Bohr developing his first quantum model of the atom.

Bohr was at the heart of the development of quantum theory, alongside de Broglie, Heisenberg and Schrödinger. He had no time for Einstein's concerns about the nature of this powerful but mysterious theory. Einstein hated the idea that probability was at the heart of quantum theory, believing that somewhere there were buried fixed values, so-called hidden variables. He sprang traps on Bohr when they met at conferences, preparing complex thought experiments that Einstein believed demonstrated flaws in the theory. Bohr would usually take the day to think through the problem and come back with a solution after tea. The last and greatest challenge came in the form of the EPR paper, which Bohr never fully challenged, but eventually experimental evidence would prove Einstein wrong.

Bohr had the habit of pacing around, muttering words as he assembled a sentence in his head. Once, at the Institute of Advanced Study he was walking around his office declaiming 'Einstein' as he pondered a quantum argument when Einstein himself slipped into the room to borrow some of Bohr's tobacco. As Einstein crept to the desk, Bohr turned to face him with a sudden, loud 'Einstein!' only to see his subject standing in front of him. Abraham Pais, who observed the event said 'There they were, face to face, as if Bohr had summoned him forth. It is an understatement to say that for a moment Bohr was speechless.'

For many years Bohr headed up the Institute of Theoretical Physics in Copenhagen, renamed the Niels Bohr Institute shortly after his death in 1962. There he worked on the nature of quantum theory, continuing to advance physics. Though he was shy, and sometimes difficult to understand, Bohr inspired a whole generation of students to carry forward our understanding of nature.

Brian Clegg

EPR

the 30-second theory

Einstein could not accept the 'Copenhagen' view that quantum objects might have some properties that are undefined until they are measured. In 1935 he and two colleagues, Boris Podolsky and Nathan Rosen, published a paper showing how that view led to an apparently untenable paradox. They imagined a quantum process that produced two particles whose states are correlated – indelibly related to one another. According to the Copenhagen interpretation, the two correlated particles don't actually have fixed values of the property in question – it could be the polarization state of two photons, say – until we look. The very act of looking at one *determines* the state of the other. But how can the measurement of one photon instantaneously make its effect felt on the other? We could in principle leave the measurement until the two correlated particles were vast distances apart. Then it's as if some influence or signal has been transmitted instantly across that distance. But according to special relativity, nothing can travel faster than light. Schrödinger coined a word for this correlated state of two particles in the Einstein-Podolsky-Rosen (EPR) thought experiment: entanglement. In the 1980s an experimental investigation using laser photons prepared in entangled states proved that EPR correlations do exist.

3-SECOND THRASH

The Einstein-Podolsky-Rosen experiment was a thought experiment designed to show that abandoning a 'realist' view of quantum properties leads to an apparent paradox.

3-MINUTE THOUGHT

The reason EPR correlations don't in fact violate Einstein's special relativity is that, although measurement on one particle does essentially fix the state of the other, that state can never be firmly established without conveying information from one particle's location to the other, which can't happen faster than light. The particles don't really 'communicate'; rather, their properties have to be considered as not 'localized' on the particles themselves. This is called quantum nonlocality.

RELATED ENTRIES

See also
HIDDEN VARIABLES
page 98

ENTANGLEMENT TRIUMPHS
page 104

3-SECOND BIOGRAPHIES

BORIS PODOLSKY
1896–1966
Russian-American physicist who worked with Einstein at Princeton, and acted as a Soviet spy, passing on information about American nuclear science during the Second World War

NATHAN ROSEN
1909–95
American-Israeli physicist whose work on general relativity led to the hypothesis of an 'Einstein-Rosen' bridge in spacetime – later dubbed a wormhole

30-SECOND TEXT

Philip Ball

A measurement on an entangled particle will have an instant effect on its twin however far apart the two are separated.

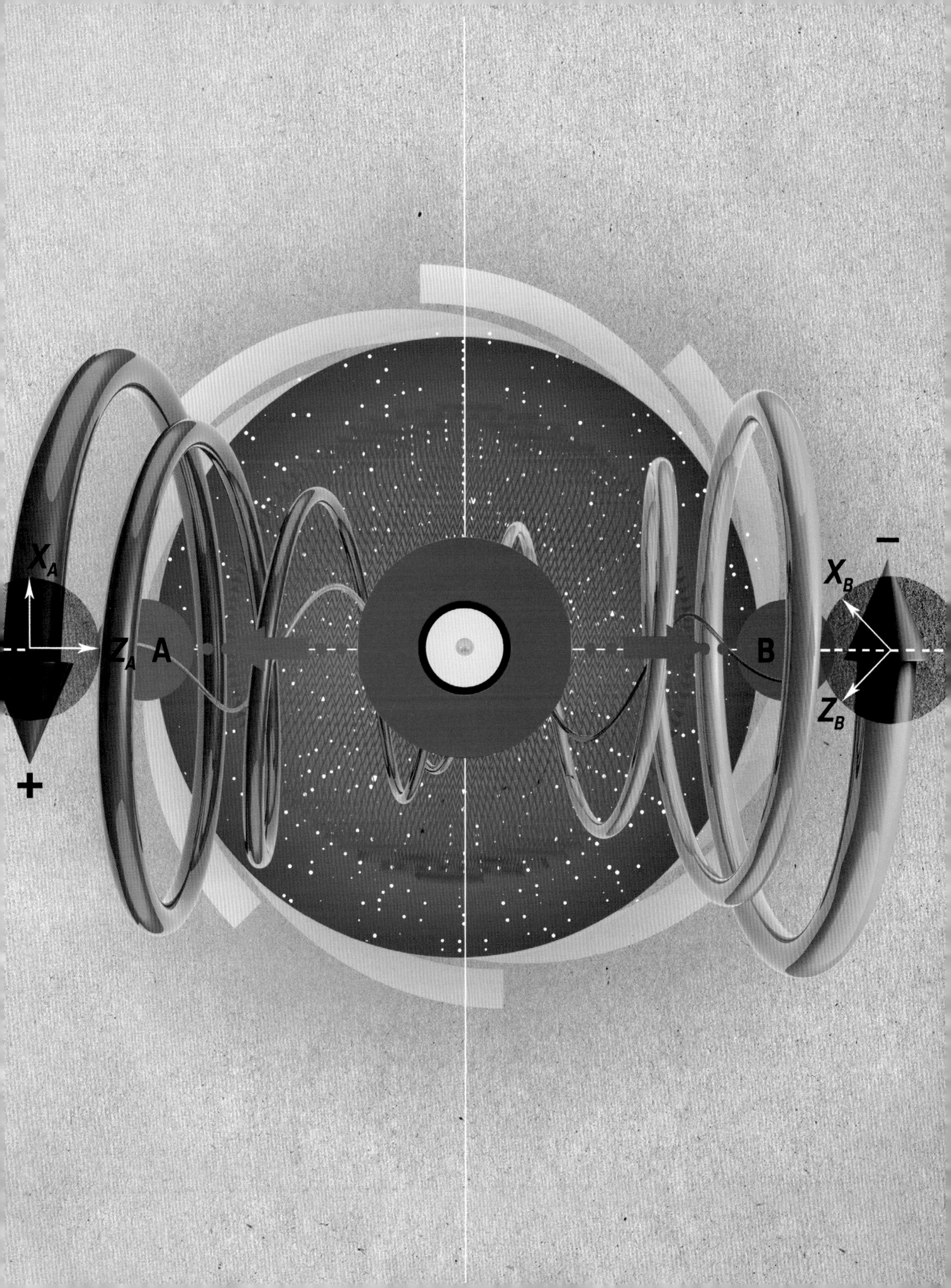

X_A
Z_A
A
+
B
−
X_B
Z_B

ENTANGLEMENT TRIUMPHS

the 30-second theory

With EPR, Einstein thought he had issued an unbreakable challenge to the validity of quantum physics. But two physicists made it possible to show that Einstein was wrong experimentally. The first was John Bell, who wrote a little-read paper showing a way to make an indirect measurement that would demonstrate whether entangled particles really could influence each other at a distance, or whether there were hidden variables. The second, Alain Aspect, came across Bell's paper while taking three years off from physics as an aid worker in Cameroon. On his return to France, Aspect devised an experiment producing entangled photons, which made measurements in different directions millions of times a second, a requirement to use Bell's concept. These changes were made so fast that there wasn't time for information to get from one photon to another – so when they demonstrated the kind of communication that is produced by entanglement, it showed that the information somehow got from A to B instantaneously. Many experiments since have tested the effects of entanglement in ways that would not allow for conventional means of communication, and they conclusively show that entanglement and quantum weirdness exists.

3-SECOND THRASH
Despite Einstein's certainty that EPR would bring quantum physics down, a theoretical test and experimental verification showed that entanglement existed and there were no hidden variables.

3-MINUTE THOUGHT
Aspect's experiment required photon detectors to change direction millions of times a second. This was mechanically impractical and so instead he used the way that the refractive index of water changes when water is put under pressure to redirect photons as they passed into the fluid, hitting one detector when under pressure and a detector at a different angle when not. The pressure change was caused by vibrating transducers, a variant of the devices that power loudspeakers.

RELATED ENTRIES
See also
HIDDEN VARIABLES
page 98

EPR
page 102

REALISM & REALITY
page 106

3-SECOND BIOGRAPHIES
JOHN BELL
1928–90
Northern Irish physicist working at CERN who devised a test to demonstrate if hidden variables existed

ALAIN ASPECT
1947–
French physicist who was the first to demonstrate definitively that quantum entanglement works as predicted by quantum theory

30-SECOND TEXT
Brian Clegg

French physicist Alain Aspect devised an experiment that would test John Bell's predictions and proved entanglement is real.

P_1
V_1
V_1
P_1
S
P_2
V_2
V_2
P_2

REALISM & REALITY

the 30-second theory

Philosophers and mystics have long maintained that the reality we perceive is not really there. But quantum theory seems to insist on something far stranger: that it is meaningless to ask about what is 'there' until we look. Pascual Jordan, who worked with Niels Bohr to define the quantum worldview in the 1920s, claimed that 'observations not only disturb what has to be measured, they produce it … We compel [a quantum particle] to assume a definite position.' But isn't this the antithesis of science, which assumes an objective reality that we can probe with experiments? That's why Einstein was uncomfortable with this kind of quantum reality. He once expressed his worries by asking if the Moon exists only when we look at it. He told his friend Max Born 'that the description of quantum mechanics … has to be regarded as an incomplete and indirect description of reality'. He suspected that there were 'hidden variables' that always awarded particles definite states even if we couldn't measure them. But experiments conducted since the 1970s have made it ever harder to construct any kind of hidden-variable theory consistent with what we observe, and most physicists now reject the idea. As far as the Moon is concerned, it seems that *something* is there when we don't look, but exactly what is determined by our looking.

3-SECOND THRASH
Einstein could not accept the notion proposed by some other pioneers of quantum theory that we determine what the world is like by the act of looking – he maintained that there must be a fixed underlying reality.

3-MINUTE THOUGHT
One of the puzzling aspects of quantum theory is how our classical world, with objects in particular places and states, emerges from the underlying quantum physics. This quantum-classical transition is now largely explained via decoherence, whereby the 'quantumness' of the system leaks away because of its interactions with its environment – interactions that become more pronounced and complex as the system gets bigger. So decoherence, rather than size per se, produces classical physics.

RELATED ENTRIES
See also
EINSTEIN'S SLIT
page 94

HIDDEN VARIABLES
page 98

EPR
page 102

3-SECOND BIOGRAPHIES
MAX BORN
1882–1970
German physicist and quantum pioneer who corresponded extensively with Einstein and acted as his sounding board for thoughts on quantum realities, ethics and much else

PASCUAL JORDAN
1902–80
German physicist who also worked with Born and Heisenberg on the detailed implications of quantum mechanics

30-SECOND TEXT
Philip Ball

Given the dependence of quantum effects on an observer, Einstein asked if the Moon was there if there was no one to see it.

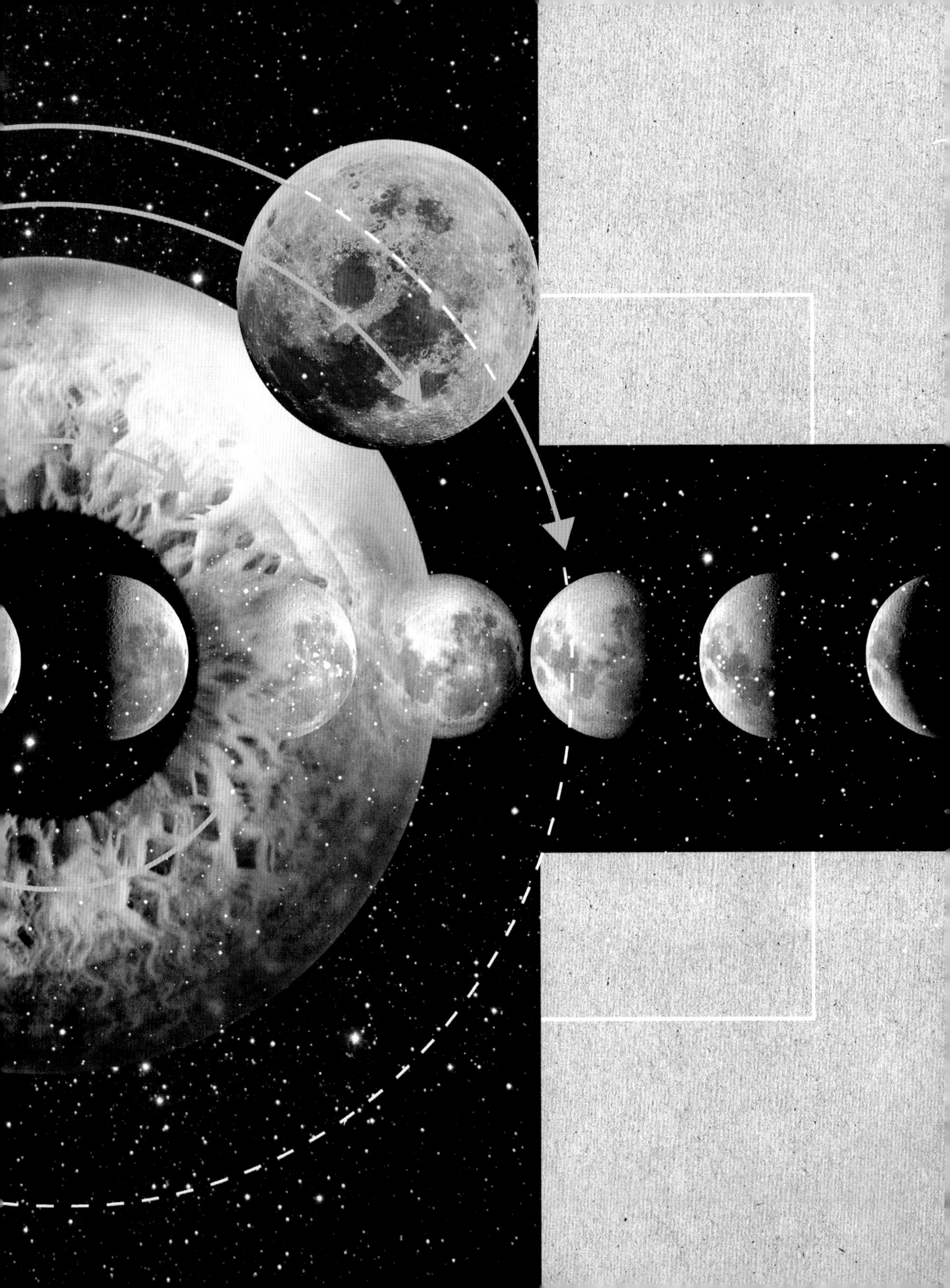

GENERAL THEORY OF RELATIVITY

GENERAL THEORY OF RELATIVITY
GLOSSARY

absolute elsewhere Because light speed is an absolute speed limit, if one thing is to influence another, it must be possible for a beam of light to get from the first thing to the second in the available time. For example, imagine a bomb two light years from Earth that can be deactivated by laser. The bomb is set to detonate in one year's time. This makes it impossible to deactivate the bomb before it explodes. In such a circumstance, the explosion is in the 'absolute elsewhere' of the Earth.
The absolute elsewhere for an event is the region of spacetime that light cannot reach, so there can never be a causal connection between the initial event and that point in spacetime.

arrow of time Spacetime makes time another dimension alongside the three spatial dimensions. But time is different. It has a clear direction pointing from past to future, the arrow of time. Many physical processes are reversible – they would run in either time direction. But the second law of thermodynamics, which says that entropy in a closed system (the level of disorder in the system) stays the same or rises, provides a clear arrow of time that explains why, for instance, you can't un-mix milk from a cup of tea.

black hole The result of an ageing star collapsing in on itself to the extent that nothing can resist the collapse and the entire star ends up as a dimensionless point. Black holes were one of the first predictions from Einstein's general theory of relativity, and though they have never been directly observed, there is good indirect evidence for their existence. Get close enough to a black hole and spacetime warps so much that even light cannot get out.

calculus Independently developed by Newton and Leibniz, calculus is a mathematical tool for analyzing change in two broad forms: differential calculus covers rates of change and relative change, while integral calculus can be used to calculate sums across ranges of values and the area, volume, etc. of geometric shapes. Calculus is central to physics and widely applicable when numbers vary systematically.

differential equations Differential equations link something to its derivatives, which are the results of applying differential calculus. They typically express the rate at which something is changing, or how one variable quantity varies with respect to another.

general covariance Physicists prefer physical laws to be generally covariant – meaning that, for instance, however you move compared to the system being studied, the laws are unchanged. This is not the case for special relativity, as it only applies in 'inertial frames of reference' – when the system being observed is in steady motion compared with the observer. General relativity takes away the need for a particular reference frame, so has general convariance.

matrix A two-dimensional array of numbers or other mathematical items, which can be manipulated using special operations to undergo arithmetical procedures like addition and multiplication.

spacetime In special relativity, Einstein showed a relationship between space and time that made it impossible to regard each separately, making it useful to consider a four-dimensional entity comprising three dimensions of space and another of time. For general relativity, Einstein then had to consider that objects with mass warped spacetime, requiring an analysis of the curvature in spacetime.

tensor calculus Calculus was modified in the 19th century to handle changes in parts of a complex equation (partial differentiation) and changes in vector fields, where each point in a multidimensional space can have both a value and direction (vector calculus). Even this was not enough for general relativity, for which Einstein had to employ tensor calculus. Tensors are mathematical structures, usually in the form of a matrix, that show how different vectors and numbers relate to each other, and tensor calculus applies to a field in which each point in multidimensional space has an associated tensor.

BREAKING INERTIAL FRAMES

the 30-second theory

Special relativity can describe situations involving objects that are either stationary or moving in a straight line at a constant speed with respect to an observer. Both the observer and the object are said to occupy inertial frames of reference. However, it is more difficult to use special relativity to describe a situation where a force is acting on an object to change its speed or direction of travel, such as an object falling in a gravitational field. The object will now be in an accelerating frame of reference. In special relativity an accelerating frame of reference must be treated differently to an inertial frame of reference. The physical equations of special relativity do not take the same form in an accelerating frame as they do in an inertial frame. By rewriting the equations of special relativity using non-linear coordinate systems it is possible to deal with an accelerating frame of reference and, for example, describe the motion of particles moving in electric and magnetic fields. However, special relativity is founded on the principle that the speed of light is constant for all observers and this is not necessarily the case when the equations of special relativity are applied to accelerating frames of reference. General relativity was born out of Einstein's attempts to apply the principles of special relativity to acceleration and gravity.

3-SECOND THRASH
Special relativity breaks down in situations involving accelerated motion and gravity.

3-MINUTE THOUGHT
What's in a name? Special relativity was not called 'special relativity' at the time when Einstein published his initial paper, entitled 'On the electrodynamics of moving bodies'. It was only later, as Einstein developed a generalized theory of relativity to deal with the limitations of his earlier work, that the name special relativity came into use. Why? Because, as Einstein wrote, 'special relativity applies to the special case of the absence of a gravitational field'.

RELATED ENTRIES
See also
ON THE ELECTRODYNAMICS OF MOVING BODIES
page 56

HERMANN MINKOWSKI
PAGE 60

A CURVE IN SPACE & TIME
page 118

3-SECOND BIOGRAPHIES
GALILEO GALILEI
1564–1642
Italian astronomer who was the first to realize that the laws of the universe should be the same everywhere – that is, in all reference frames

ISAAC NEWTON
1643–1727
English physicist whose laws of motion established the idea of inertial frames of reference

30-SECOND TEXT
Leon Clifford

To a steadily moving observer, the laws of physics are unchanged, but when accelerating this no longer holds true.

y
y′
v
O
x
x′
z′
13

THE HAPPIEST THOUGHT

the 30-second theory

Einstein's starting point for general relativity was what he later called his 'happiest thought', which came to him while working at the Swiss patent office. Einstein realized that if someone falls, say, off a high building, his or her acceleration cancels out the pull of gravity. They are weightless. (Aircraft in free fall, so-called 'vomit Comets', simulate this to give experience of weightlessness.) The two things – acceleration and gravity – are indistinguishable in their effects: this is the 'equivalence principle'. The implication was that if, for instance, you were in a spaceship with no windows and it was under constant acceleration, you would be pushed towards the rear of the craft, just as we are pushed into our seats when a plane accelerates down the runway. But if the same spaceship were sitting rear end down on a planet where the gravitational pull produced the same acceleration, you would also be pulled the same way towards the rear and would not be able to distinguish from your position in the spaceship whether you were accelerating or sitting still on the planet. This equivalence between acceleration and gravity would prove essential in understanding the way that gravity is produced as a warp in space and time.

3-SECOND THRASH

In his 'happiest thought' Einstein realized that acceleration and gravity are indistinguishable in their effects, which would lead on to his ideas on the nature of gravity itself.

3-MINUTE THOUGHT

Einstein said 'I was sitting in a chair in the patent office at Bern when all of a sudden a thought occurred to me: "If a person falls freely he will not feel his own weight." I was startled. The simple thought made a deep impression on me. It impelled me toward a theory of gravitation.' This is why astronauts in orbit float around. They are in free fall towards Earth, but also move sideways, so miss the surface.

RELATED ENTRIES

See also
FROM PATENTS TO RELATIVITY
page 52

BREAKING INERTIAL FRAMES
page 112

3-SECOND BIOGRAPHIES

GALILEO GALILEI
1564–1642
Italian natural philosopher who discovered the earlier equivalence principle that steady motion is indistinguishable from being motionless

ABRAHAM PAIS
1918–2000
Dutch-American physicist and Einstein biographer who shared Einstein's 'happiest thought' remark, quoting an unpublished paper

30-SECOND TEXT

Brian Clegg

The observation that a person who is falling feels no gravity, seen in vomit Comets and space stations, inspired Einstein's 'happiest thought'.

HEAVY CLOCKS

the 30-second theory

Einstein predicted that gravity would slow down time. To see how this works we need to imagine two people – Alice and Ben – in a rocket that is accelerating, with Alice at the front and Ben at the back. Alice and Ben send light pulses between each other, and by measuring how much time elapses between each pulse they can each measure how quickly time is passing. Suppose that Alice sends two light pulses to Ben, and that she measures a time interval between sending the two pulses. Ben receives the two pulses at the back of the rocket; but because of the rocket's acceleration the time interval between receiving the two pulses will be less than the time interval Alice measured between sending them. Suppose Alice measures her pulses to be 2 seconds apart, Ben may measure them to be only 1 second apart. Time will appear to pass more slowly for Ben than it does for Alice: his seconds last twice as long. From the principle of equivalence, what is true for an accelerating rocket is also true for a rocket stationary in a gravitational field. If the rocket were standing vertically on the surface of a planet, Ben's clock would tick *more slowly* than Alice's, because he is in a stronger gravitational field. So, gravity slows down time.

3-SECOND THRASH
Einstein's principle of equivalence tells us that clocks will run slower in a stronger gravitational field; so clocks on Earth run slower than clocks orbiting on the International Space Station.

3-MINUTE THOUGHT
The Global Positioning System (GPS), which we use in our sat-navs, has to take account of the fact that a clock on Earth will run slower than a clock in a satellite because it is in a stronger gravitational field. If we did not correct for this effect, the system would give us incorrect positions and would be useless.

RELATED ENTRIES
See also
LENGTH, TIME & MASS
page 64

THE HAPPIEST THOUGHT
page 114

A CURVE IN SPACE & TIME
page 118

3-SECOND BIOGRAPHY
JOSEPH HAFELE
1933–2014
American physicist who, along with his colleague Richard Keating, in 1971 flew atomic clocks aboard commercial aeroplanes to test Einstein's two predictions of time dilation in special relativity and time passing more quickly in a weaker gravitational field

30-SECOND TEXT
Rhodri Evans

In an accelerating ship, a clock slows down: the same effect should be (and is) observed with gravity.

A CURVE IN SPACE & TIME

the 30-second theory

Special relativity has limitations when dealing with acceleration and gravity. However, Einstein believed that the laws of physics should apply in all circumstances including systems in accelerated motion and in the presence of gravitational fields. This means that equations and physical measurements such as time and distance, velocity and acceleration should be consistent – or, in mathematical language, covariant – between different frames of reference and in all systems of coordinates. The trouble was that the mathematics of special relativity run into problems with Euclidean geometry. The mathematical constant Pi, for example, would appear to change on an imaginary spinning disc due to the effects of special relativity shrinking the circumference of the disc. The solution to this problem, suggested by mathematician Marcel Grossman, was to adopt a non-Euclidean geometry to frame the principles of relativity. Euclidean geometry rests on the axiom that the shortest distance between two points is a straight line. In a non-Euclidean geometry, space becomes curved and the shortest distance between two points is a path across the curved surface – known as a geodesic. Einstein and Grossman's key insight was to represent gravity as a curvature in non-Euclidean spacetime, i.e., they saw that gravity is curved spacetime.

3-SECOND THRASH
By thinking of gravity as a curvature in the fabric of spacetime, Einstein overcame the limitations imposed by special relativity.

3-MINUTE THOUGHT
Think of spacetime as two-dimensional, like one side of a piece of paper. The familiar three dimensions of space are squashed into one dimension running parallel with one side. Time runs at right angles. Objects with mass sit on the paper. This is the spacetime of special relativity. Replace the paper with a rubber sheet. Objects with mass sink into the sheet – deforming and curving it in a new dimension. This is the spacetime of general relativity.

RELATED ENTRIES
See also
ON THE ELECTRODYNAMICS OF MOVING BODIES
page 56

HERMANN MINKOWSKI
page 60

3-SECOND BIOGRAPHIES

GEORG FRIEDRICH BERNHARD RIEMANN
1826–66
German mathematician who developed non-Euclidean geometry – essentially, the geometry of curved space

MARCEL GROSSMAN
1878–1936
Hungarian mathematician who introduced Einstein to the idea of non-Euclidean curved-space geometries

30-SECOND TEXT
Leon Clifford

The presence of a massive body like the Sun warps spacetime so that an object like the Earth moving in a straight line follows a curved path.

28 December 1882
Born in Kendal in the English Lake District

1902
Graduates from Owens College, Manchester with a BSc degree

1903
Awarded a mathematics scholarship at Trinity College, Cambridge

1905
Gains his master's degree from Cambridge University

1906
Obtains a post as chief assistant at the Royal Observatory in Greenwich

1907
Elected a fellow of Trinity College, Cambridge

1913
Becomes Plumian Professor of Astronomy at Cambridge

1914
Promoted to director of the Cambridge Observatory

1916
Exempted from military service during the First World War

1919
Measures the deflection of starlight during a solar eclipse

1923
Produces a textbook on *The Mathematical Theory of Relativity*

1928
Publishes his best-known book, *The Nature of the Physical World*

1930
Receives a knighthood from King George V

22 November 1944
Dies in Cambridge

qualified to understand Einstein's notoriously difficult theory. He gained a first-class degree in physics in 1902, at the age of just 19, followed three years later by an MA in mathematics. By the time he was 24, however, he was working not as a physicist or mathematician but as an assistant astronomer at the Royal Greenwich Observatory. By combining his three areas of expertise – physics, mathematics and astronomy – he soon became one of Britain's foremost astrophysicists. In 1914 he was elected fellow of the Royal Society and director of Cambridge University observatory.

Like Einstein, Eddington was a committed pacifist. When compulsory conscription was introduced in 1916, he obtained an exemption on the grounds that his work in astrophysics was of national importance. Whether this was true or not is debatable, but the scientific importance of his work was indisputable: it ranged from investigating the internal constitution of stars to looking at the dynamics of star clusters. 1916 was also the year that to Brazil and a remote African island during the eclipse of May 1919. Six months later, after Eddington had carefully analyzed the results, the Royal Society announced that Einstein's theory had been vindicated. To the astonishment of everyone – not least Eddington and Einstein – the press loved this offbeat news story and it was soon making headlines around the world. Wittingly or not, Eddington had given birth to Einstein-mania.

Eddington remained an outspoken champion of relativity for the rest of his life. His textbook on *The Mathematical Theory of Relativity* was praised by Einstein, shortly before his death, as 'the finest presentation of the subject in any language'. Eddington also wrote popular science books such as *The Nature of the Physical World*, coining memorable terms like 'the arrow of time' and 'absolute elsewhere' in an attempt to get Einstein's complex ideas across to a general readership. By the time he died in 1944, he was Sir Arthur Eddington, having been knighted in 1930.

Andrew May

NEEDING A NEW MATHEMATICS

the 30-second theory

General relativity requires non-Euclidean geometry and a curved spacetime that cannot be described using conventional mathematics. This could have been a major stumbling block for the development of a generalized theory of relativity. Fortunately, in the course of the 19th century, mathematicians had been developing exactly the kind of mathematics that Einstein needed. General relativity requires the manipulation of complicated arrays of values similar to matrices that are called tensors. A matrix can describe a mathematical transformation mapping one state to another within a Euclidean space. Tensors can describe such transformations in non-Euclidean spaces with the greater flexibility needed to cope with the changing curvature of spacetime caused by gravitational fields. Tensors are complex mathematical objects that behave in peculiar ways. They need a bespoke notation to describe them and the theory of calculus must be extended to handle them. The properties of tensors, the notation needed to describe them and the rules of calculus to manipulate them had all been worked out by the time Einstein needed them. With Marcel Grossman's help, Einstein mastered the techniques of tensor calculus sufficiently to express his theory as a set of elegant mathematical equations.

3-SECOND THRASH
General relativity was such a groundbreaking theory that Einstein needed a different kind of mathematics in order to describe the physics in the form of equations.

3-MINUTE THOUGHT
Physicists have a habit of finding uses for apparently obscure ideas in pure mathematics. James Clerk Maxwell's equations pushed imaginary numbers into service. Einstein discovered a use for non-Euclidean geometries and tensor calculus. Paul Dirac applied a highly specialized form of algebra that has been built on by modern theorists. Some physicists believe there is a deep relationship between mathematics and reality. What new discoveries in physics may lurk in the existing theorems of pure mathematics?

RELATED ENTRIES
See also
A CURVE IN SPACE & TIME
page 118

THE EQUATIONS
page 126

3-SECOND BIOGRAPHIES
ELWIN BRUNO CHRISTOFFEL
1829–1900
German mathematician and physicist who created a notation for describing the tensors used in general relativity

WOLDEMAR VOIGT
1850–1919
German physicist and mathematician who applied the term tensor to the complicated matrix-like mathematical objects used in general relativity

30-SECOND TEXT
Leon Clifford

The equations of general relativity make use of the geometry of curved space and multidimensional objects called tensors.

W. Voigt,
man in U, V, W resp.
x mit ξ = xm₁ + yn₁ + zp₁ − αt
y mit η = xm₂ + yn₂ + zp₂ − βt
z mit ζ = xm₃ + yn₃ + zp₃ − γt
t mit τ = t − (ax + by + cz)
und bezeichnet die ... Functionen resp. mit (U), (V),
v = (V), w = (W) ebenfalls
von ihnen:
Die Differentialgleichung
worin ω die Fortpflanzung
die Fortpflanzungsgeschwin
Amplitude — bezeichnet.
Relation erfüllen:
und diese ist, da ja sein muß:
erfüllt, wenn folgende neue Gleichungen bestehen:
Es seien nun u = U, v = V, w = W
Gleichungen, welche an einer gegebenen Oberfläche
C₁
C₂
C₃
σ₂
σₙ
½(σ₁ − σ₂)
½(σ₂ + σ₃)
½(σ₁ + σ₃)
T^(e₃)
e₃
σ₃₃
σ₃₁
σ₃₂
σ₁₃
σ₁₂
σ₂₁
σ₂₂
σ₂₃
e₂
T^(e₁)
T^(e₂)
x₁
x₂
x₃
σ₁₁
cos⁻¹ a₁₃
cos⁻¹ a₂₁
x′₁
x′₂
3)
σ′₁₁
σ′₁₂
σ′₁₃
σ′₃₁
σ′₃₂
σ′₂₁
σ′₂₂
σ′₂₃

THE HILBERT CHALLENGE

the 30-second theory

Einstein was not the only person working on the problem of general relativity; German mathematician David Hilbert was also on the case. Hilbert was fascinated by the mathematical challenge of expressing physical laws in an invariant form – so they remain the same in all circumstances. This means they work in all frames of reference and, unlike special relativity, do not depend on a particular system of coordinates; a property called general covariance. Hilbert pursued the mathematical challenge of seeking generally covariant equations for relativity. Where Einstein tackled this as a physics problem, Hilbert's approach built up from mathematical axioms. Hilbert and Einstein knew each other, were in communication and were well aware of each other's work. They completed their respective derivations of the field equations of general relativity virtually simultaneously. Hilbert submitted a draft of his paper in 1915 ahead of Einstein's submission but Einstein's paper appeared first. Einstein had done much of the groundwork on general relativity but Hilbert had been first to figure out how to solve the crucial final step. There remains uncertainty about how much the two men influenced each other and whether Hilbert's work helped Einstein crack the problem. Hilbert never claimed credit for general relativity.

3-SECOND THRASH
German mathematician David Hilbert derived the field equations of general relativity at almost the same time as Einstein.

3-MINUTE THOUGHT
Physics was ripe for the emergence of relativity at the turn of the 20th century. Many mathematicians and physicists were working on the ideas that Einstein successfully fused. There is little doubt that, even without Einstein's huge intellectual effort, someone would have discovered relativity. So,if history had taken a slightly different turn, we could now be talking about Hendrik Lorentz's theory of special relativity and David Hilbert's theory of general relativity.

RELATED ENTRIES
See also
A CURVE IN SPACE & TIME
page 118

NEEDING A NEW MATHEMATICS
page 122

THE EQUATIONS
page 126

3-SECOND BIOGRAPHIES
ERNST MACH
1838–1916
Austrian physicist whose view that the large-scale structure of the universe affects physical laws influenced Einstein's approach

DAVID HILBERT
1862–1943
Outstanding German mathematician who helped structure the modern concepts of mathematics

30-SECOND TEXT
Leon Clifford

Einstein raced against the great German mathematician, David Hilbert, to be the first to complete the general theory of relativity.

$\sqrt{-g} = 1$

THE EQUATIONS

the 30-second theory

In a series of four papers published in late 1915 Einstein outlined his theory of general relativity. These culminated with a short paper entitled *Die Feldgleichungen der Gravitation* ('The Field Equations of Gravitation'), which contained a workable mathematical formulation of general relativity. The paper sets out a tensor relationship that yields a set of ten equations that Einstein describes as generally covariant; that is, they will hold true anywhere, in all frames of reference and in any coordinate system. Mathematically, the equations can be written as a set of non-linear partial differential equations. They describe the curvature of spacetime. The equations are consistent with the fundamental physical laws of the conservation of energy and the conservation of momentum. The fact that they are non-linear means they cannot always be solved; for example, in a situation where there is strong and changing curvature of spacetime – such as two black holes orbiting one another. The equations can be simplified where the gravitational field is very weak and space is not curved to be consistent with special relativity. The equations are equivalent to Newton's laws when gravitational fields are weak and velocities are significantly less than the speed of light.

3-SECOND THRASH

Ten related equations form the core of general relativity, which describes how the gravitational field due to the presence of mass and energy curves spacetime.

3-MINUTE THOUGHT

Einstein showed that general relativity resolved an astronomical mystery that had been puzzling scientists. The orbit of the planet Mercury did not behave as it should according to Sir Isaac Newton's laws. The point where Mercury's orbit passes closest to the Sun, known as the perihelion, moves around the Sun – or precesses – fractionally faster than it should do according to Newton's laws. Einstein's equations precisely account for this mysterious variation in the precession of Mercury's orbit.

RELATED ENTRIES

See also
BLACK HOLES
page 134

THE COSMOLOGICAL CONSTANT
page 140

UNIFIED FIELD THEORIES
page 150

3-SECOND BIOGRAPHIES

ISAAC NEWTON
1643–1727
English physicist and mathematician whose laws of motion described the orbits of the planets around the Sun

GEORGE FRANCIS ELLIS
1939–
South African physicist who discovered new solutions to the field equations with cosmological implications

30-SECOND TEXT

Leon Clifford

The first success of Einstein's equations was in perfectly predicting the difference in the orbit of Mercury from Newton's theory.

Die Feldgleichungen der Gravitation.

EDDINGTON'S EXPEDITION

the 30-second theory

According to Einstein's theory of curved spacetime, the light from a distant star should be bent by a small but measurable amount as the light ray passes close to the Sun. Under certain assumptions Newton's theory also predicts a deflection of light, but only by half the amount. Thus it ought to be possible to discriminate between the two theories by measuring the actual amount of bending, and in 1916 Einstein issued a challenge to astronomers to do just that. There was a catch, though: the necessary observations had to be made during a total solar eclipse, which is the only time stars are visible close to the Sun. The next suitable eclipse was due on 29 May 1919, when the path of totality stretched from South America to equatorial Africa. The British astronomer Arthur Eddington organized two expeditions, sending one team to Sobral in Brazil, while his own team headed for the island of Principe off the coast of Africa. Despite a series of frustrating problems – including cloudy skies at Principe and excessively hot weather at Sobral – the expeditions were ultimately successful, and Eddington was able to claim victory for Einstein.

3-SECOND THRASH
The first experimental confirmation of Einstein's theory of general relativity came in 1919, when Eddington measured the deflection of starlight during a total solar eclipse.

3-MINUTE THOUGHT
Although it was widely accepted at the time that Eddington's observations supported Einstein's theory over Newton's, they were actually far from being conclusive. All the photographs were degraded, and in most cases the margin of error encompassed both Einstein's prediction and Newton's. The average deflection came out very close to Einstein's value, but only because Eddington discarded measurements that disagreed with his expectations. Later measurements confirmed Einstein's theory with far greater certainty.

RELATED ENTRIES
See also
A CURVE IN SPACE & TIME
page 118

GRAVITATIONAL LENSES
page 136

3-SECOND BIOGRAPHY
ARTHUR EDDINGTON
1882–1944
English astrophysicist, science popularizer and champion of general relativity

30-SECOND TEXT
Andrew May

Arthur Eddington used observation of the shift in position of stars seen near to the eclipsed Sun to test general relativity.

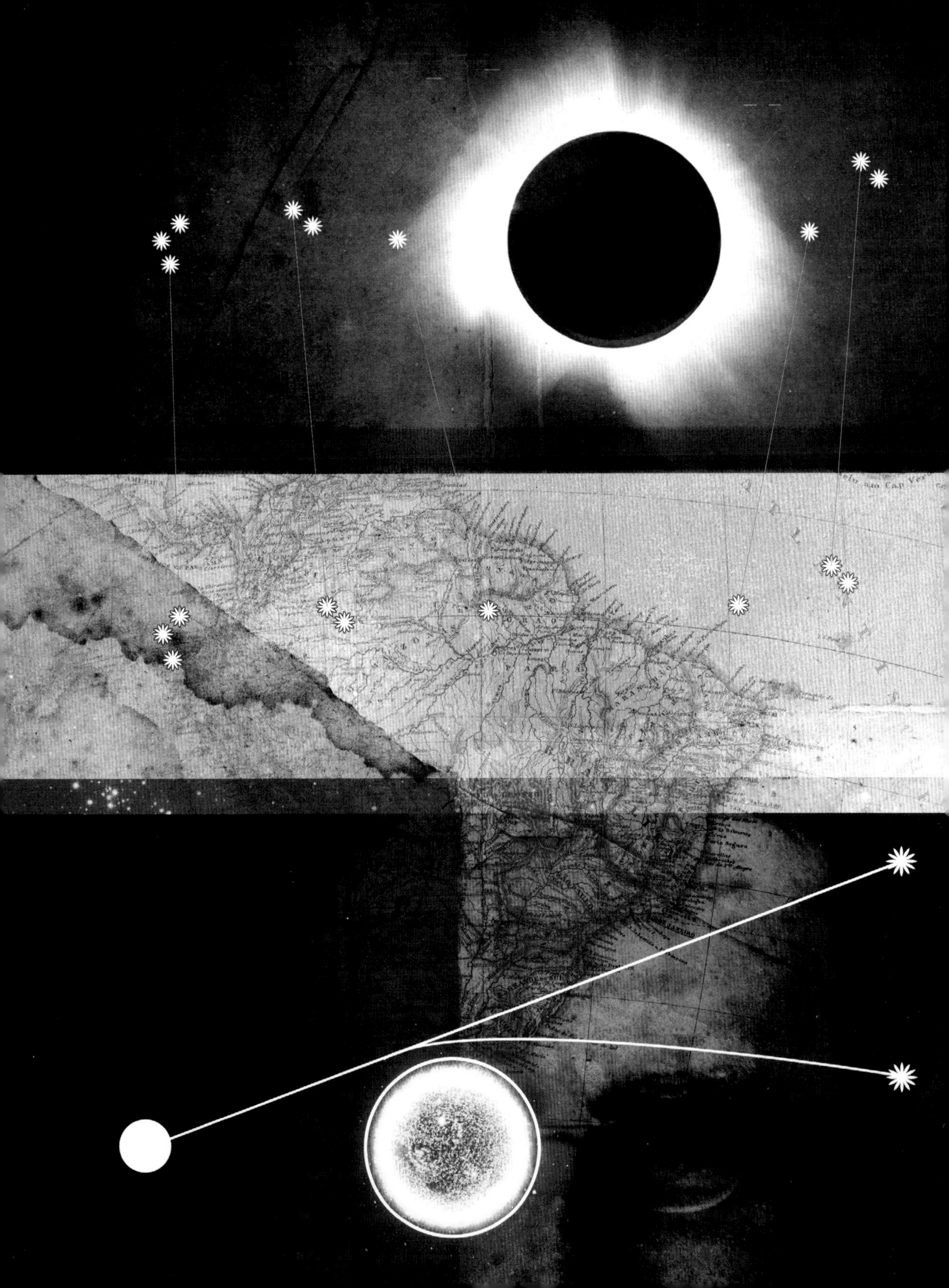

EINSTEIN'S UNIVERSE

BICEP2 detector Based at the South Pole, the BICEP (Background Imaging of Cosmic Extragalactic Polarization) 2 detector is a sensitive electromagnetic detector used to study the polarization of the cosmic microwave background radiation.

binary pulsar A pulsar is a fast rotating neutron star – a very dense collapsed star – that emits regular electromagnetic pulses from a lighthouse-like beam of radiation that sweeps around as the star rotates. Some pulsars have a companion star. Such binary pulsars have a pulse rate that increases and decreases in a cycle, making them a potential source of gravitational waves.

cosmic microwave background radiation Around 380,000 years after the big bang, the universe cooled sufficiently to form uncharged atoms, allowing light to flow freely for the first time. Since then, this light has continued to travel. Probes designed to detect this ancient radiation show a near-uniform distribution in all directions, with tiny fluctuations thought to reflect the early variation in density that seeded the galaxies.

cosmological constant When Einstein produced his gravitational field equations they showed that the universe should expand. He put in a constant, represented by the Greek letter *lamda* (Λ) to add extra gravitational attraction to stop this happening. A modified value of this constant represents the dark energy thought to cause acceleration in the expansion of the universe.

dark energy It has been known since the early 20th century that the universe is expanding. Recently, however, it has also been discovered that this expansion is accelerating. Such an acceleration needs *something* to drive it, and this something is described as dark energy. There is, as yet, no good explanation for this. Dark energy accounts for around 68 per cent of the mass/energy in the universe.

dark matter Dark matter is a hypothetical substance that only interacts with other matter by gravity. With no electromagnetic interaction, it can't be seen and passes through ordinary matter undetected. The existence of dark matter is inferred from astronomical phenomena, notably the way that galaxies spin so fast that, were there not large amounts of undetectable matter present, they would fly apart. There is estimated to be around five times as much dark matter as normal matter in the universe, accounting for 27 per cent of the total mass/energy.

interferometry Measurement using interference between two light beams. When light beams of the same frequency are brought together after travelling down different paths, the waves will either reinforce, making a bright region, or cancel, leaving it dark. By sending beams of light down different long paths at right angles to each other, scientists can search for small variations in the environment that influence those beams by the shift in the interference pattern.

quasi-stellar object Quasi-stellar objects, or quasars, are extremely bright sources of electromagnetic radiation that are very distant, yet often brighter than an entire galaxy. Quasars are thought to be the radiation given off as material is drawn into a supermassive black hole at the heart of a distant, young galaxy – most date back more than 12 billion years.

singularity If a star collapses to form a black hole, the resultant entity is a singularity, where the entire mass of the star ends up as an infinitely dense point. Singularities are highly speculative, as current physics breaks down under those conditions.

supernova A supernova is a stellar explosion, far brighter than the original star, giving off the equivalent of the lifetime output of a star in a few months. Supernovae occur when a massive star collapses, or when an old star pulls in extra material (for example, from another star that orbits it), triggering a thermonuclear explosion. Some supernovae make good 'standard candles' to determine the location of distant galaxies.

weak nuclear force There are four forces of nature: the strong and weak nuclear forces, electromagnetism and gravity. The weak nuclear force is involved during nuclear fission and radioactive decay, and often results in the transformation of a quantum particle into one or more other quantum particles.

BLACK HOLES

the 30-second theory

Even in the 18th century scientists appreciated that the gravitational field of a very massive object, such as a big star, could be too strong to allow light (then thought to be composed of particles) to escape. But when Einstein's theory of general relativity supplanted Newton's gravitational theory in the early twentieth century, the truth looked even stranger. When a large star runs out of fuel so that it no longer radiates the energy that buoys up its mass, the equations predicted that it would collapse under its own gravity to phenomenal densities. Above a certain mass limit, nothing can prevent the collapse from continuing until all the mass is concentrated in an infinitesimally small dot called a singularity. The gravitational field then curves the surrounding spacetime into a region from which nothing can escape, not even light. Anything approaching within a certain distance of the collapsed star – the event horizon – is doomed to get sucked inside and crushed out of existence. The idea seemed too absurd to be generally accepted until general relativity became an area of intense research in the 1960s, when these objects were christened black holes. Astronomical observations now strongly support the idea that most galaxies have supermassive black holes at the centre. But a full theory of them awaits the unification of quantum physics with a theory of gravity.

3-SECOND THRASH

Black holes are extinct massive stars that have collapsed under their own gravity into a (theoretically) infinitely dense point, from which no light can escape.

3-MINUTE THOUGHT

British physicist Stephen Hawking argued in the 1970s that black holes are not really black, nor are they cosmic dead ends. Because of quantum effects at their event horizon, they are predicted to radiate energy, which gradually depletes their mass until eventually they may evaporate. This Hawking radiation has not yet been detected. Hawking's theory also predicts the existence of mini black holes weighing just a few micrograms.

RELATED ENTRIES

See also
SPACETIME
page 66

WORMHOLES
page 144

3-SECOND BIOGRAPHIES

SUBRAHMANYAN CHANDRASEKHAR
1910–95
Indian astrophysicist who pioneered the theory of stellar gravitational collapse and defended it against much undue criticism and ridicule

JOHN WHEELER
1911–2008
American theoretical physicist, central to the renaissance of general relativity in the later 20th century, who allegedly coined the name 'black hole'

30-SECOND TEXT

Philip Ball

Black holes were one of the first predictions of general relativity: a star that warped spacetime so much that even light could not escape.

GRAVITATIONAL LENSES

the 30-second theory

3-SECOND THRASH
Because they curve spacetime, foreground objects can act as gravitational lenses of background objects, forming multiple images and magnifying them.

3-MINUTE THOUGHT
Gravitational lensing provides a way to measure the mass of objects, and is one of the main pieces of evidence supporting the theory that much of the mass of galaxies and clusters of galaxies is in the form of invisible dark matter. We can use the lensing produced in different parts of a galaxy cluster to map out the distribution of dark matter.

One of the first experimental verifications of general relativity came in 1919, when Arthur Eddington showed that gravity bends light in agreement with Einstein's equations. In 1924 Orest Chwolson suggested that the light from a background source could appear as an arc around a foreground object, with the foreground object acting as a gravitational lens. This effect was quantified by Einstein in 1936, and in 1937 Fritz Zwicky suggested that galaxy clusters might act as gravitational lenses to background objects, producing an observable effect. This was first observed in 1979 when twin quasi-stellar objects (quasars) were discovered, each having the same red shift. Initially thought to be two separate objects, it was realized after careful analysis that observers were seeing two gravitationally lensed images of the same quasar, the lensing being produced by a foreground cluster of galaxies. By the mid-1990s gravitational lensing by individual galaxies was being observed, a phenomenon termed microlensing. Unlike a normal lens, with a gravitational lens maximum bending occurs closest to the centre of the lensing object, and the amount of lensing can be used to measure the mass of the lensing object. Also, just like with a normal object, gravitationally lensed objects can be magnified and this has allowed us to see distant objects that would otherwise be too dim to detect.

RELATED ENTRIES
See also
A CURVE IN SPACE & TIME
page 118

EDDINGTON'S EXPEDITION
page 128

3-SECOND BIOGRAPHIES
OREST CHWOLSON
1852–1934
Russian physicist who, in 1924, was the first person to publish an article about gravitational lenses

FRITZ ZWICKY
1898–1974
Swiss astronomer who suggested, in 1937, that clusters of galaxies could produce observable gravitational lensing. He also was the first to suggest the existence of dark matter, also in 1937

30-SECOND TEXT
Rhodri Evans

Massive objects like a galaxy can warp light around it like lens, sometimes producing multiple images of the same object.

GRAVITATIONAL WAVES

the 30-second theory

When Einstein developed his theory of general relativity in 1916, he quickly discerned a remarkable consequence. Just as electromagnetic waves, like light and radio waves, are generated when electrical charges oscillate, so the movements of massive objects with strong gravitational fields should induce ripples in spacetime as their mass distorts it. In other words, they should excite gravitational waves, in which spacetime is compressed and extended. The amplitude of such quakes would only be detectably large if the bodies in question were extremely massive and their motions violent: for example, if a star explodes in a supernova or two black holes collide. Gravitational waves were largely seen as a curiosity until the 1960s, when it became apparent that they could open a window for observing such extreme events in the cosmos, just as radio and X-ray astronomy disclose new astrophysical objects. Detecting them is extremely difficult, as they would be likely to induce spacetime deformations of just 10^{-18} m or so. But detectors are now searching for these waves via the changes they would produce in the interference of light beams travelling repeatedly back and forth along tubes a few kilometres long. No gravitational waves have yet been seen, but most researchers are confident that this will happen eventually.

3-SECOND THRASH

Gravitational waves are ripples in spacetime, predicted by general relativity and caused by violent astrophysical events involving extremely massive objects.

3-MINUTE THOUGHT

The big bang, in which the universe formed, should have produced 'primordial' gravitational waves. These would not now be detectable directly, but it is predicted that they left an imprint in the pattern of cosmic microwave background radiation, the afterglow of the big bang. A claimed detection of that fingerprint in 2014, using the BICEP2 detector at the South Pole, caused great excitement but later proved to be false.

RELATED ENTRIES

See also
A CURVE IN SPACE & TIME
page 118

BLACK HOLES
page 134

GRAVITATIONAL LENSES
page 136

3-SECOND BIOGRAPHIES

RAINER WEISS
1932–
German-American physicist who proposed that interferometry might be used to detect gravitational waves

JOSEPH HOOTON TAYLOR
1941–
American astronomer whose discovery and observations of a binary pulsar in the 1970s supplied indirect evidence for gravitational waves

30-SECOND TEXT

Philip Ball

Gravity wave detectors use extremely long light beams at right angles to each other to attempt to detect distortions in spacetime.

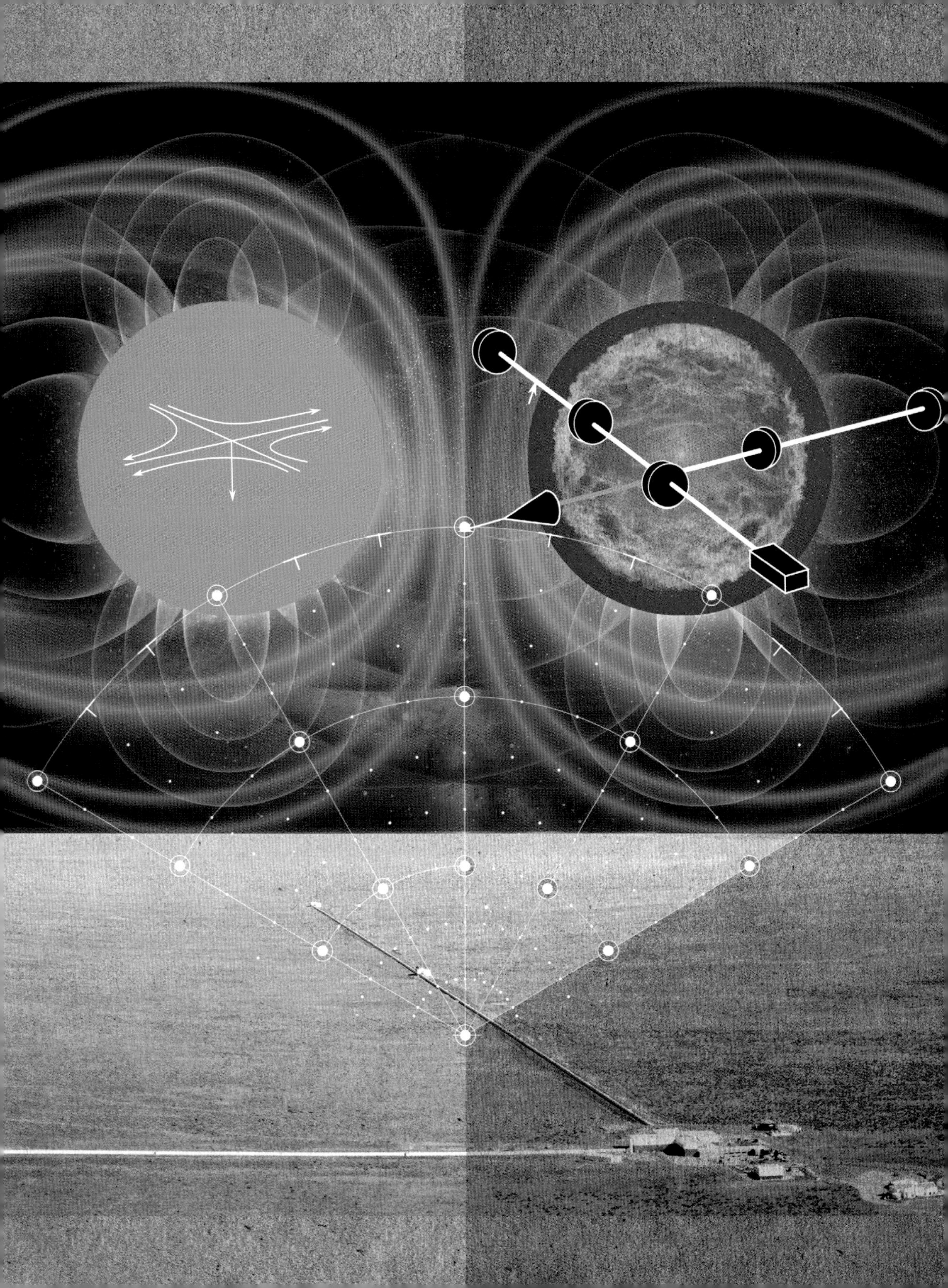

THE COSMOLOGICAL CONSTANT

the 30-second theory

3-SECOND THRASH
Einstein introduced the cosmological constant to produce a static Universe, but today the force implied by the constant may explain why its expansion is accelerating.

3-MINUTE THOUGHT
If dark energy is identified with the cosmological constant, then its strength is a property of space itself. We have found evidence that when the Universe was less than half its current age its expansion was indeed slowing down, but as space expanded the effect of the cosmological constant became dominant and the expansion started to accelerate. Theories predict that the Universe's expansion will continue to get quicker and quicker.

In 1917 Einstein realized that his theory of gravity predicted a non-static Universe. At the time the prevailing opinion was that the Universe was static; Einstein therefore introduced the cosmological constant – an extra value incorporated into his general relativity equations that adds a theoretical force counteracting the attraction of gravity and making the Universe static. In 1929 Edwin Hubble discovered that the Universe was expanding, and this led to Einstein abandoning the idea of the cosmological constant and referring to his introduction of it as the biggest blunder of his life. The idea of the cosmological constant remained largely abandoned until the 1990s. However, in 1998 two teams announced the surprising discovery that the expansion of the Universe was getting quicker. They had been trying to measure the expansion rate of the Universe today compared to when it was about half of its current age; everyone expected it to have slowed due to gravity. Instead, they found that the expansion rate of the Universe is quicker now than in the past; this accelerating expansion is attributed to dark energy. Although there are other candidates, the most popular explanation for dark energy is Einstein's cosmological constant.

RELATED ENTRIES
See also
A CURVE IN SPACE & TIME
page 118

GRAVITATIONAL LENSES
page 136

EXPANDING UNIVERSES
page 142

3-SECOND BIOGRAPHIES
EDWIN HUBBLE
1889–1953
American astronomer who, in 1929, showed that the speed at which galaxies are receding from us is directly related to their distance from us

MICHAEL TURNER
1949–
American theoretical astrophysicist and one of the champions of the case for the cosmological constant, who coined the term 'dark energy'

30-SECOND TEXT
Rhodri Evans

American astronomer Edwin Hubble detected the expansion of the universe, which was subsequently discovered to be accelerating.

EXPANDING UNIVERSES

the 30-second theory

In the 1910s Vesto Slipher, working at the Lowell Observatory in Arizona, found from the Doppler shift of their light that most spiral nebulae were moving away from us. By the early 1920s Edwin Hubble had shown that spiral nebulae were, in fact, galaxies beyond our own Milky Way. In 1929 Hubble found that more distant galaxies were moving away more quickly: a galaxy twice as far away is moving away twice as fast. The simplest explanation of this is that the Universe is expanding, with all galaxies moving away from one other. Ever since this discovery the question has been: Will the Universe's expansion continue forever, or will the attractive force of gravity eventually stop its expansion and cause it to collapse? This question seems now to have been answered, with the discovery in 1998 that the expansion is not slowing down as everyone expected, but is instead speeding up. The speeding up is often attributed to the cosmological constant, a repulsive component of gravity that Einstein introduced in 1917. As space expands, the cosmological constant will dominate more and more, leading to the Universe expanding at an ever-increasing rate, with no obvious mechanism for the acceleration to stop.

3-SECOND THRASH
The future of our expanding Universe is not known, but recent evidence suggests that the expansion will continue and get quicker due to the cosmological constant.

3-MINUTE THOUGHT
If the Universe's expansion continues to accelerate then the light from other galaxies will ultimately become so red-shifted that their light will become unobservable. Even individual galaxies, stars and atoms may be torn apart, in something called the big rip.

RELATED ENTRIES
See also
A CURVE IN SPACE & TIME
page 118

BLACK HOLES
page 134

3-SECOND BIOGRAPHIES
GEORGES LEMAÎTRE
1894–1966
Belgian mathematician who first proposed that the Universe began in an explosion from an initially very dense state – the big bang

ADAM RIESS
1969–
American astrophysicist who used supernovas as standard candles to measure the expansion rate of the Universe

30-SECOND TEXT
Rhodri Evans

Depending on the rate of expansion, the universe could eventually contract again, continue to expand as it is, or accelerate.

WORMHOLES

the 30-second theory

Wormholes, also known as Einstein-Rosen bridges, may be popular in science fiction – and may not exist in reality – but the general theory of relativity makes them possible in principle. Dreamed up in the 1930s, a wormhole makes use of the kind of distortion that a black hole makes in spacetime to link one point in the universe to another. A common illustration of a wormhole is to consider spacetime as a two-dimensional sheet (obviously there are other dimensions, but we are setting those aside for the illustration) that is folded back on itself. Getting from a point halfway along the top half of the folded sheet to a point halfway along the bottom half would normally involve traversing half the length of the sheet. However, if it were possible to burrow through from top fold to bottom fold, the distance disappears. In principle, a black hole linked to its inverted equivalent, a white hole, could distort spacetime to provide this kind of ability, provided it were possible to travel through the wormhole unscathed. As yet, with the possible exception of the big bang, we have no evidence for white holes existing, but it is an entertaining possibility.

3-SECOND THRASH
A wormhole is a hypothetical application of general relativity, originally called an Einstein-Rosen bridge, which links two distant points via a warp in spacetime.

3-MINUTE THOUGHT
If a wormhole existed, relativity predicts that it would collapse before anything could pass all the way through it. To keep the bridge open would require negative energy – similar to the dark energy thought to be causing the expansion of the universe. If wormholes existed, by moving one end rapidly while keeping the other fixed, it would be possible to generate a relativistic time differential, creating a time machine that would make it possible to travel backwards in time.

RELATED ENTRIES
See also
A CURVE IN SPACE & TIME
page 118

BLACK HOLES
page 134

FRAME DRAGGING & TIME TRAVEL
page 146

3-SECOND BIOGRAPHIES
NATHAN ROSEN
1909–95
American-Israeli physicist, one of the three contributors to the EPR paper and the main originator of the Einstein-Rosen bridge concept

KIP THORNE
1940–
American physicist specializing in general relativity and its astrophysics consequences, including wormholes

30-SECOND TEXT
Brian Clegg

A wormhole provides a hypothetical link between two points in spacetime as a result of distortion of spacetime by bodies.

FRAME DRAGGING & TIME TRAVEL

the 30-second theory

When Einstein produced his field equations for general relativity he had to take into account some secondary effects. One emerged from special relativity, which showed that when an object is moving, because of its change in mass, it produces a small gravitational effect at right angles to its motion of travel. If the moving object rotates, this effect is called frame dragging. It's a bit like twisting a spoon in a jar of honey. As the spoon rotates it pulls the nearby honey with it, creating a miniature vortex. Similarly, frame dragging pulls the surrounding spacetime with a rotating body. If a very massive object, like a cylinder constructed from neutron stars, could be rotated very quickly, it has been suggested that spacetime would be so distorted that it would be possible to travel backwards in time by looping around the rotating body. American physicist Ronald Mallett has suggested that frame dragging using circling laser beams (which also produce a small frame dragging effect) could produce a tiny time displacement in the laboratory. Others dispute Mallett's use of theory and whether the lasers could produce a big enough effect. As yet the idea has not been experimentally verified.

3-SECOND THRASH

Frame dragging is a secondary effect in general relativity producing a small gravitational pull at right angles to a moving body that could produce a spacetime vortex when a body rotates.

3-MINUTE THOUGHT

Frame dragging was confirmed by NASA's longest-running project. Gravity Probe B was planned in 1962, launched in 2004 and delivered its first results in 2011. The experiment used four rotating quartz spheres coated in niobium – the most perfectly spherical man-made objects to date – as gyroscopes to detect the effect. By 2011 a later experiment had already demonstrated frame dragging and Gravity Probe B lost its NASA funding, but private funding enabled the experiment to be completed.

RELATED ENTRIES

See also
BREAKING INERTIAL FRAMES
page 112

A CURVE IN SPACE & TIME
page 118

WORMHOLES
page 144

3-SECOND BIOGRAPHIES

FRANCIS EVERITT
1934–
English-born Stanford physicist whose life's work was the Gravity Probe B project

RONALD MALLETT
1945–
American physicist whose work in general relativity has led him to a possible approach to fulfil a childhood dream of building a time machine

30-SECOND TEXT

Brian Clegg

When a massive body rotates, the effect of frame dragging causes it to pull spacetime around with it.

9 July 1911
Born in Jacksonville, Florida

1927
Wins a scholarship to Johns Hopkins University in Baltimore

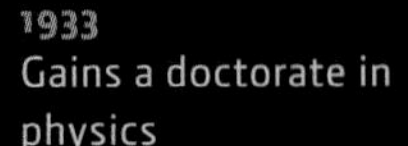

1933
Gains a doctorate in physics

1934
Moves to Copenhagen to work with Niels Bohr

1938
Becomes assistant professor of physics at Princeton University

1942
Joins the Manhattan Project, helping to develop the atomic bomb

1945
Returns to Princeton after the war

1949
Is called back to government work, this time on the hydrogen bomb

1967
Popularizes the term 'black hole'

1973
Co-authors *Gravitation*, a huge textbook on general relativity

1976
Becomes director of theoretical physics at the University of Texas

1986
Returns to Princeton as emeritus professor

1988
Receives the Einstein Medal from the Albert Einstein Society

13 April 2008
Dies in Hightstown, New Jersey

JOHN WHEELER

John Archibald Wheeler helped to bring Einstein's theory of general relativity, for many years considered an obscure niche subject, into the mainstream of physics – and he made famous one of its best-known consequences: 'black holes'.

The young Wheeler was something of a prodigy, earning a university scholarship at 16 and a doctorate at 21. A year later he was in Copenhagen, working alongside one of the greatest figures of twentieth-century physics, Niels Bohr. In 1938, he was appointed assistant professor of physics at Princeton, and thus found himself in the same town as Einstein, who had been a member of Princeton's Institute for Advanced Study since 1933. The two became good friends, and Wheeler occasionally held seminars with his students at Einstein's house.

Wheeler's main interest during the early part of his career was nuclear physics, and in 1939 he co-wrote a paper with Niels Bohr on the mechanism of nuclear fission. This interest inevitably led to his involvement in the Manhattan Project, aimed at developing a practical atomic bomb. Wheeler was stationed at the Hanford Site in Washington state, where he helped design nuclear reactors to produce the isotopes needed for the bomb.

Wheeler returned to Princeton after the war, but was called back to government service in 1949 – this time to work on the even more powerful hydrogen bomb. One strand of this work, called Project Matterhorn, was taking place there in Princeton, so Wheeler was free to pursue his academic career in parallel with the government work. In the early 1950s he began to teach a course on general relativity – something that was almost unheard-of at the time. He also had frequent discussions with the ageing Einstein about the possibility of a 'unified field theory', by which general relativity might be extended to encompass electromagnetic forces as well as gravity.

It was through Wheeler's efforts that general relativity gradually found its way into mainstream physics teaching – and, in one aspect at least, into the popular imagination. It has frequently been said that Wheeler was the first to use the term 'black hole' in 1967; however, it was used by someone else at an American Association for the Advancement of Science meeting in 1964: we're not sure who. But Wheeler was responsible for its widespread use. He remained a strong advocate of Einstein's theory for the remainder of his long life – he died at the age of 96 in 2008.

Andrew May

UNIFIED FIELD THEORIES

the 30-second theory

Einstein's two great contributions to physics – the idea of quanta and the theory of general relativity – are not compatible. One led to the theory of quantum mechanics, which accurately describes the universe on a very small scale. The other is a theory of gravitation that successfully describes the universe on a very large scale. Both quantum mechanics and general relativity explain forces such as electromagnetism and gravitation in terms of fields but the two theories cannot be melded together. Einstein spent many years trying to do this without success and modern physicists are still working on the problem. Special relativity was successfully combined with quantum mechanics in 1928 by the great physicist Paul Dirac. This was followed in the 1970s by the inclusion of the weak nuclear force. But all attempts to bring gravity into the fold have failed. Physicists have been unable to quantize the gravitational field described by the equations of general relativity in the same way as they have done for the electromagnetic field described by the equations of James Clerk Maxwell. Physicists hypothesize a particle of quantum gravitational force – the graviton – analogous to the photon, which is a quantum of electromagnetic force; but so far no one has found a graviton. The quest continues.

3-SECOND THRASH
A unified field theory combining general relativity with quantum mechanics is the Holy Grail of physics – and like the Holy Grail, it remains unfound.

3-MINUTE THOUGHT
Einstein once quipped in relation to his ideas about quantized vibrations that 'everything is vibration'. There may have been more truth to that statement than he realized at the time. Some physicists believe so-called string theories may help unify quantum mechanics with general relativity. These theories describe particles as tiny vibrating strings with different modes of vibration producing different types of particle. In this model, the entire universe is made from vibrating strings.

RELATED ENTRIES
See also
THE EQUATIONS
page 126

GRAVITATIONAL WAVES
page 138

JOHN WHEELER
page 148

3-SECOND BIOGRAPHIES
JAMES CLERK MAXWELL
1831–79
Scottish physicist who unified electricity, light and magnetism

PAUL DIRAC
1902–84
English physicist who unified special relativity with quantum mechanics to create quantum electrodynamics (QED)

30-SECOND TEXT
Leon Clifford

Quantum theory successfully explains the very small, while general relativity explains large scale gravity, but the two are not compatible.

n1
n2
n3
n4
n 5

APPENDICES

RESOURCES

BOOKS

Albert Einstein: Pocket Giants
Andrew May
(The History Press, 2016)

Antimatter
Frank Close
(Oxford University Press, 2010)

Before the Big Bang
Brian Clegg
(Saint Martins Griffin, 2011)

A Brief History of Time
Stephen Hawking
(Bantam Books, 1995)

The Collected Papers of Albert Einstein
Albert Einstein et al.
(Princeton University Press, 1987)

Einstein: His Life and Universe
Walter Isaacson
(Simon & Schuster, 2007)

Einstein's Miraculous Year
Roger Penrose, Albert Einstein, and John Stachel
(Princeton University Press, 2005)

The Elegant Universe
Brian Greene
(Vintage, 2000)

The God Particle: If the Universe is the answer, what is the question?
Leon Lederman
(Mariner Books, 2006)

The Grand Design
Stephen Hawking
(Bantam Books, 2010)

Quantum: A Guide for the Perplexed
Jim Al-Khalili
(Weidenfeld & Nicolson, 2004)

Physics of the Impossible
Michio Kaku
(Anchor Books, 2009)

The World As I See It
Albert Einstein
(Filiquarian Publishing, 2007)

Why Does $E=mc^2$?
Brian Cox and Jeff Forshaw
(Da Capo, 2010)

MAGAZINES/ARTICLES

Beyond Einstein
Scientific American, September 2004
www.scientificamerican.com

Dark Energy: Was Einstein right all along?
New Scientist, December 3, 2005
www.newscientist.com

Einstein [In a nutshell]
Discover, September 2004
www.discovermagazine.com

Einstein's Blunders
Focus, July 2010
www.bbcfocusmagazine.com

Person of the Century
Time, June 14, 1999
www.time.com

WEB SITES

The Albert Einstein Society
www.einstein-bern.ch

American Institute of Physics: Einstein Exhibit
www.aip.org/history/einstein/

Einstein Archives Online
www.alberteinstein.info

Einstein Papers Project
www.einstein.caltech.edu

Eric Weisstein's World of Physics
scienceworld.wolfram.com/physics/

Frequently Asked Questions in Physics
math.ucr.edu/home/baez/physics/

Large Hadron Collider
www.lhc.ac.uk

LISA Gravitational Wave Observatory
lisa.nasa.gov

NOTES ON CONTRIBUTORS

EDITOR

Brian Clegg read Natural Sciences, focusing on experimental physics, at the University of Cambridge. After developing hi-tech solutions for British Airways and working with creativity guru Edward de Bono, he formed a creative consultancy advising clients ranging from the BBC to the Met Office. He has written for *Nature*, the *Times*, and the *Wall Street Journal* and has lectured at Oxford and Cambridge universities and the Royal Institution. He is editor of the book review site www.popularscience.co.uk, and his own published titles include *A Brief History of Infinity* and *How to Build a Time Machine*.

CONTRIBUTORS

Philip Ball is a freelance writer, and was an editor for Nature for more than 20 years. Trained as a chemist at the University of Oxford, and as a physicist at the University of Bristol, he writes regularly in the scientific and popular media, and has authored books including *H2O: A Biography of Water*, *Bright Earth: Art and the Invention of Colour*, *The Music Instinct: How Music Works and Why We Can't Do Without It*, and *Curiosity: How Science Became Interested in Everything*. His book *Critical Mass: How One Thing Leads to Another* won the 2005 Aventis Prize for Science Books. He has been awarded the American Chemical Society's Grady–Stack Award for interpreting chemistry to the public, and was the inaugural recipient of the Lagrange Prize for communicating complex science.

Leon Clifford is a writer and a consultant and a business director whose speciality is simplifying complexity. Leon has a BSc in physics-with-astrophysics and is a member of the Association of British Science Writers. He worked for many years as a journalist covering science, technology and business issues with articles appearing in numerous publications including *Electronics Weekly*, *Wireless World*, *Computer Weekly*, *New Scientist*, and the *Daily Telegraph*. Leon is interested in all aspects of physics – particularly climate science, astrophysics and particle physics. He is managing director of science communications business Green Ink which focuses on the challenges of communicating science for development.

Rhodri Evans studies and researches in extra-galactic astronomy. Rhodri has, for over 16 years, been involved in airborne astronomy, and is a key part of the team building the facility far-infrared camera for SOFIA. He is also involved in research into star-formation and cosmology, and is a regular contributor to television, radio and public lectures. Rhodri runs the blog www.thecuriousastronomer.wordpress.com.

Andrew May is a technical consultant and freelance writer on subjects ranging from astronomy and quantum physics to defence analysis and military technology. After reading Natural Sciences at the University of Cambridge in the 1970s, he went on to gain a PhD in Astrophysics from the University of Manchester. Since then he has accumulated more than 30 years' worth of diverse experience in academia, the scientific civil service and private industry.

INDEX

ACKNOWLEDGEMENTS

PICTURE CREDITS
The publisher would like to thank the following individuals and organizations for their kind permission to reproduce the images in this book. Every effort has been made to acknowledge the pictures; however, we apologize if there are any unintentional omissions.

Science Photo Library: 24.
Photo Researchers / Alamy Stock Photo: 44.
Bygone Collection / Alamy Stock Photo: 62.
Corbis: 80.
Archive Pics / Alamy Stock Photo: 102.
Archive Pics / Alamy Stock Photo: 122
INTERFOTO / Alamy Stock Photo: 150